"There are healing words in 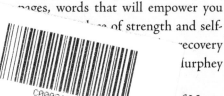 ...ages, words that will empower you and move you through pain ... ... of strength and self-confidence. For thirty years I ... ...ecovery comes when issues are faced ... Murphey will be part of that toolbox ...
—GREGORY L. ... of Hope, and ... ood Abuse

"Cecil Murphey and the other men whose testimonies in ... s book have looked into the secret places of their lives and have pulled out a powerful resource for healing wounds men seldom talk about. Unfortunately, the accounts related in this book are more common than most would want to admit, yet hiding the hurts will not heal the hurts or make the repercussions of unspoken pain go away. With each meditation, this book peels back the layers and speaks with brutal honesty about the lasting effects of sexual abuse on boys or young men. . . . Ultimately, however, this book is not merely about reliving the pain but invites the reader to heal, move forward, and even forgive and find freedom from the bondage that comes from such abuse. . . . Men need to know they are not alone, and there is a way out of the long dark night."
—MARK E. HARDGROVE, dean of Beulah Heights University, and senior pastor of Conyers Church of God

"During this unique historical moment of the #metoo movement, I can't imagine a timelier book. Having been abused myself during childhood, this book helped me heal in a more profound way. This book does more than just identify with those who have been abused: it offers hope and healing. Cecil and his friends are brave to use their lives to bring healing to others. 'Each of you should use whatever gift you have received to serve others, as faithful stewards of God's grace in its various forms' (1 Peter 4:10). This is deeply needed today not only in America but around the world."
—MARK FINCANNON, motion picture casting director

"*More Than Surviving* calls men to step into a healing community and embrace change. Through these remarkable meditations, Cecil reveals his own candid account, as well as those of five other men abused as children. Each of these brave survivors have brought their childhood secrets to light, pressed through incredible pain, uncovered lies, and learned to value themselves as individuals loved by God. The prayers at the end of each meditation may well transform your life and relationships."

—KAREN CICCARONE, cofounder of the Oasis Healing Ministry
for survivors of sexual abuse and assault

"Cecil Murphey's *More Than Surviving* talks honestly about the emotions and struggles of men who battle with the aftermath of childhood abuse. With transparency and grace, Cec and the other contributing authors write about the identity confusion, grief, guilt, betrayal, loss, stolen opportunities, and shattered trust experienced by countless men. *More Than Surviving* is a voice for men who struggle to speak their pain, offers hope for their healing, and is a testament to God's love and grace."

—SHELLY BEACH, award-winning author of *Love Letters from the Edge:
Meditations for Those Living with Brokenness, Trauma, and the Pain of Life*

"Honest. Open. Heart-wrenching. A reminder that if you or someone you love has suffered abuse, you are not alone. There is hope. There is help. Cec Murphey is more than an eloquent wordsmith; he knows that healing comes when we know someone will hear our stories and love us without reservation. When men are abused as children, masculinity suffers. Confusion reigns. Murphey reminds us that we don't live in a neat and tidy world with explanations for everything: 'Logical answers don't satisfy emotional needs.' He is living proof that God's grace breaks through our wounded past and offers light in the midst of our darkness."

—DON S. OTIS, author of *Whisker Rubs: Developing the Masculine
Identity*, and president of Veritas Communications

"Are you a victim of childhood abuse or married to a survivor? Cecil Murphey courageously addresses the fears, frustrations, and fallout that frequently linger from childhood abuse. *More Than Surviving* provides specially crafted meditations that inspire healing, peace, and a more loving connection with God. If you want to move past merely surviving the trauma of your childhood, if you want to live in the fullness God desires—pick up a copy of this book! You won't be disappointed."

—JULIE GORMAN, co-owner of Gorman Leadership Group, and coauthor
of *Married for a Purpose* and *Two Are Better Than One*

MORE THAN SURVIVING

Courageous Meditations for Men
Hurting from Childhood Abuse

CECIL MURPHEY

Kregel
Publications

Dedicated to hurting men
and the secondary survivors in their lives

— Contents —

I'm a survivor of childhood abuse—sexual, physical, and verbal. I don't know if one form was worse than the others.

Does it matter? What matters is that I hurt for a long, long time.

Like many other males, I never told anyone.

Whom would I tell? The people I should have been able to trust were the ones who violated me.

For a long time, I felt different from other men, as if something inside me hadn't been wired correctly. "What's wrong with me?" I must have asked myself that question thousands of times over the years.

Some days I felt as if I wanted to die; other days I didn't know if the struggle was worth it. I can now say it was worth the fight. I also believe the only way any of us can find healing from our stolen childhoods is to face our suffering and abuse.

I didn't face up to the reality of my abusive childhood until I hit fifty-one. The hurt and damage of the past finally broke through—slowly and with fragmented memories. Later I spoke with my three older sisters, who confirmed many of those painful memories.

I had been fondled regularly by a female relative until I was about four or five years old. When I was six or seven, an elderly man rented a room in our house. He sexually assaulted me and my sister, who was four years older. She told on him. Dad beat up the man, threw him out of the house, and threatened to kill him if he saw him again.

My father was also an alcoholic—a brutal one when he was drunk, which he was every weekend. Out of seven children, two of us became his primary targets for regular beatings. On the days he didn't beat me, he berated me by calling me useless and lazy.

With that kind of background, I sometimes wonder how I lived within the range of normalcy. I had almost no religious training as a child, so God wasn't part of my conscious life. My only response is that, even then, God was with me and took me through that horrendous time.

When I was ready to face my past, two people accepted my brokenness.

My late wife, Shirley, and my best friend, David, lovingly supported me, allowed me to cry, and reminded me that they loved me.

Later I met other men who had been victimized as children, and as I disclosed my pain, they entrusted me with their stories. Many of us found healing through talking with other survivors.

It took me years to be able to speak openly about the molestation. Since then I've been reaching out to hurting men, pointing them to inner healing. In 2010, I started a blog called *Shattering the Silence* (www.menshattering thesilence.blogspot.com). Many of those once-assaulted men have impacted me with their stories and candid responses. I give freely and receive gladly from their open hearts. We have become an online healing community. This book is a result of that community.

✦   ✦   ✦

At the end of each chapter, you will read a short prayer. Each petition sums up the chapter. I urge you to repeat the words aloud. You may not *feel* the words, but they're true, so please say them anyway. Pause from time to time and repeat the words over again.

If you were an abused male (or a woman who loves a once-abused male), I wrote this book for you.

For healing.

For peace.

For a stronger, more loving connection to the God who created you and loves you.

> God, help me know you love me and remind
> me that you want to heal my pain.

— *My Contributors* —

I asked eight men to contribute to this book. I made it clear that I wanted to use their names and that they were free to add any personal information they chose. My purpose was to publish what they said (with minor editing) to encourage other male survivors to speak up. I also wanted readers to see that this isn't only my personal experience.

Of the eight, three men turned me down and I understood and wasn't surprised. I respect their decisions, and I didn't use any of their material.

The five men who agreed are Mark Cooper, Roger Mann, Gary Roe, Tom Scales, and Dann Youle. They have allowed me to use their names as they tell their stories and share their ongoing agony. They're willing to let the world know about their painful molestation and their subsequent growth, and I applaud them.

Although they wrote the entries that bear their names, I wrote the prayers at the end of each meditation.

❉   ❉   ❉

For all other names that appear in this book, the essential story is true, but I have changed the individual's name and sometimes a few details to protect the person's privacy.

WHEN I WAS A BOY . . .

"When I was a boy . . ."

That's where my story begins; that's where many of *our stories* begin.

I was a child, and I was innocent. I trusted someone and that person stole my trust, my innocence, and my childhood. I've suffered because of the actions of another person. No matter how caring, kind, or warm the perpetrator may have appeared to be, he took advantage of me.

What I've written above is probably your story as well.

If we can focus on our childhood and realize how immature and inno-cent we were, we can also remind ourselves that we couldn't reason the way we do today as adults. We may also have taken the guilt on ourselves for what happened. If so, we need to remind ourselves: *I was a child and the abuser was a perpetrator. He (or she) took advantage of my innocence and youth.*

If we're typical, we've already gone through (or are now going through) a period of questioning and doubting. And while vague, often-terrifying mem-ories occasionally intrude, deep inside something nags at us. In our most vulnerable moments, we know the truth that someone stole our innocence.

One of the reasons for writing this book is to remind myself and others that we're not the only ones. I knew I wasn't the only victimized kid, but I *felt* as if I were.

Many of us have been where you have been or where you are now. We've felt the same kinds of pain you have. More than just having been there, we have survived and are still overcoming the trauma.

In the early days of healing, many of us need to remind ourselves a hun-dred times a day that someone victimized us. Or it might be easier to say, "Someone older and more powerful took advantage of my innocence and youth."

We need to do it because we want to convince ourselves that we didn't make up the stories. It did happen to us. And we need to tell ourselves that we won't start a sentence with the words, "I should have . . ."

Let's go back to the beginning and start with, "When I was a boy . . ." That beginning can help us learn to become kind and compassionate to ourselves.

We need to remind ourselves that we didn't know how to cope with such seductive assaults—especially when it was someone we trusted and one who whispered, "I love you and I won't hurt you."

Now we may choose to say, "When I was a boy, he lied to me." Or "When I was a boy, she bribed me, called me special." Or "He made me feel loved and wanted—temporarily."

We were wanted, but for his needs and not ours. Today we hurt because in childhood we were victimized.

You might say, "When I was a boy, I was molested. Now I'm an adult, and I'm healing from my childhood trauma."

God, I'm tired of hurting. Help me to accept
the truth about my painful childhood.

IT REALLY ISN'T TRUE

Dann Youle wrote something for my blog that I've savored because he said it well and the message echoed words I could have spoken. Most of this is the way he sent it to me in 2010.

◆　◆　◆

When I first discovered (uncovered or whatever you want to call it) that I had been sexually abused as a boy, in my head I heard myself saying, "But it really isn't true!"

Denial was *such* a defense in those early days. For twenty-eight years I had been able to deny I'd been abused, so because I thought I recalled something now, did that suddenly make it true?

This was the beginning of what I thought was my going crazy. I felt split off from myself: I didn't know who I was and the denial was the only way I could survive. I sometimes wondered if I would or could take my next breath. It was the wildest, weirdest feeling.

One day these thoughts raced through my head:

It really isn't true.
It really isn't true.
It *really* isn't true.
It really *isn't* true.
It really isn't *true*!

God, you *can't* expect me to believe this and you *can't* expect me to live if it *is* true!

At that moment, I felt God say to me, "You don't believe it can be true, I wish it weren't—but do you believe you can breathe? I give you breath, Dann; I will breathe *for* you."

Even though it was *so* hard, at that moment I realized I was more alive than ever. I felt *such* intense pain, but all the same it was glorious. Jesus was letting me know that I didn't have to be afraid. I might be scared to death in that moment that I was going to die, but I didn't have to fear anything, even if I *did*.

I have found that this phenomenon is generally true of men who have been abused. Until we can come out of that denial and get to the pain, the healing never begins.

When I was trying to convince myself that it wasn't true, there was something I needed to be in touch with even if it was painful. It was like a gentle but persistent wake-up call that God used to point me to himself.

The it-really-isn't-true response is rare for me these days. If I have to feel the pain, there's a good reason for it. It's not that I enjoy the pain, but I find that I can find Jesus in the middle of it. He feels my pain and understands pain himself. When I think of where my sin put him, I know that he has felt my pain in ways that I can't even begin to imagine. To know the depths of pain, he has allowed me to trust him more and more in the depths of my pain.

So yes, it really *is* true! I *was* abused—horribly, terribly, but not unredemptively. The pain my past abuse causes at times seems unbearable, but the healing is sweet and real.

True and loving God, please help me face the truth,
and accept your power in moving forward.

— *3* —

SOMETHING IS WRONG WITH ME

It remains one of the saddest, most painful meetings where I was invited to speak. A group of men who had been sexually assaulted and physically abused had recently formed and they asked me to speak to the group. I gleaned as much from them as they could have from me.

They had a check-in time and Ron said, "Something is wrong with me, and it torments me."

In the past, I had said those words to myself many times. I had finally figured out that such a statement wasn't true, and I didn't want another man to repeat such a self-indictment.

"No, you aren't wrong or bad!" I probably shouted those words. "Something wrong and bad was done to you!"

The others nodded but Ron shook his head. The tears began to fall as he said, "I liked what he did. I hated it, but I liked it."

George, the leader of the group and the one who invited me, leaned toward Ron. "You mean it was pleasurable? That you responded with an erection or that it felt good when you were abused?"

Ron nodded and more tears flowed.

Slowly and softly George explained, "That's an automatic, physiological response. Whenever you stimulate the penis, you get an erection. That doesn't make you a pervert."

I marveled at the compassion in his voice as he tried to make Ron realize that his reaction had been normal. And he spoke healing words for several of the men who nodded and smiled. One of them said, "Thank you for saying that. I didn't have the courage to say those words."

George wasn't saying we were perfect or flawless. He meant that the men had problems, but that didn't make them blemished or worthless.

Loving God, you created me lovable. Remind me of that
today. And tomorrow. And all my days afterward.

17

IT'S NOT FAIR

When I was a member of a recovery group sponsored by the State of Georgia, one man cried out during the second meeting, "It's not fair!" He went on to compare himself with his older and younger brothers who, seemingly, were not molested and had no serious problems.

After allowing him to rant for several minutes, the therapist said, "You're right. It's not fair, but it is real."

Dean, the quietest man in the group, pulled up his left pants leg and showed his prosthesis from just below the knee. "And this isn't fair either. It's not fair that I'm alive and my dad died in the accident."

We were stunned and hardly knew how to respond but Dean added, "You can groan all you want about the unfairness, but nothing will change. If you're willing to grow up, you'll accept the reality and ask, 'Now how do I live the rest of my life?'"

I can't remember how the exchange went after that, except the it's-not-fair complainer yelled and groaned. He never came back to the group, and he was our first dropout.

Maybe the poor man couldn't face the reality of his situation. Storming against the unfairness of life does no good. If anything, it makes it worse because we can't accept life as it is.

It took me a long time, but I finally began to say, "What is, is what is." That's my shorthand way of saying, "That's the situation and I can't change it. But now I can make decisions on what to do next."

Lord Jesus, life wasn't fair to you. It's not fair to me. Help
me accept what is and triumph over the injustices.

WHAT DID I DO TO DESERVE THIS?

I don't like it when men ask what wrong thing they did to deserve abuse. Do you catch the implication? They imply two things. First, they sinned or did something wrong and, second, the molestation was divine punishment.

That hardly makes sense to me. In the gospel of John, the disciple encountered a man born blind and asked, "Who sinned, this man or his parents, that he was born blind?" Jesus responds, "Neither this man nor his parents sinned" (John 9:1–3).

They lived in a world that believed the "curse causeless shall not come" (Prov. 26:2 KJV) and they seemed intent on finding who was the wrongdoer. Jesus dismisses their question. He reaches out to heal the man and says this will bring glory to God.

We may need to remind ourselves that we serve a compassionate and caring God—one who doesn't punish children because of the sin or evil doings of someone else. I don't serve a God who constantly throws terrible punishment on me and forces me to spend an inordinate amount of time trying to figure which of my many sins God is punishing me for or if I have to keep searching until I can blame an ancestor.

I like to keep it simple: evil people do evil things. The perpetrators may not consider their actions evil, but when they harm someone else, that's evil.

Another point is that Jesus, in defending children, said that whoever welcomes a child welcomes him (see Matt. 18:5) and then adds, "As for whoever causes these little ones who believe in me to trip and fall into sin, it would be better for them to have a huge stone hung around their necks and be drowned in the bottom of the lake" (v. 6 CEB).

I can't explain why God doesn't strike dead those who hurt children— that's beyond my grasp—but I can say, "If you were molested, this is one time you were not the problem or the cause."

Despite any shame you and I feel, we need to acknowledge and never forget that we were the innocents. Or as I sometimes say, "I did nothing bad; something bad was done to me."

> God, please don't let me blame myself for my childhood
> abuse. Help me recover through your grace and love.

WHY DOES IT HURT SO MUCH?

Early in my healing process, I asked that question repeatedly. I was hurting and I couldn't understand the reason for the intense pain. I wanted to face the reality of my traumatic childhood, learn from the experience, and move on with my life. I didn't want the pain, or at least I wanted less of it.

My real question didn't involve *why* as much as it did *how*. How do I get rid of the torment, the painful memories, and reexperiencing my childhood trauma? Like thousands of other survivors, I learned to say those now-clichéd words, *I had to feel the pain to move beyond the pain*. As memories trickled back (some exploded), I faced each one. In private, I cried often in those early days; I raged, and I yelled at my perpetrators.

In the midst of those rants and tears, I wanted relief. It did help to vent, but it helped even more to talk to the two people who loved me enough to stay with me in my pain—my wife and my friend David.

What worked for me may not be the path for everyone. We have different temperaments and see life through our personal, unique experiences. If we want healing, each of us needs to find our own way.

One suggestion—and it's advice I firmly believe—is to share our pain.

When we open up to at least one other person, someone who cares for us, healing begins to take place. We need to choose someone who will listen to us pour out our agony. We tell them, "I'm not asking for advice, only that you listen and hear my struggle."

Try it.

> God, I don't want to feel the pain; I remind myself
> that it won't last. Help me to remember that the
> more I heal, the less intensely the pain lingers.

DEFINED BY ABUSE

Sexual abuse doesn't define me, but it does define what happened to me.

I hope you'll ponder that statement. Too many have suffered and built their lives around being abused.

Some run from the thought of it or try to deny that it happened. Others put themselves in situations where they're victimized repeatedly (or they might say taken advantage of). Or they go out of their way to protect other boys from sexual assault. Although they may not say it in words, their message is, I want to be there for other boys because no one was there for me.

And some victims of abuse become perpetrators themselves. The reasons it happens are as complicated and as varied as the individuals.

But ultimately, abuse can never excuse our behavior. It is simply an explanation for how we arrived where we are.

> Loving God, remind me that sexual abuse doesn't
> define me. It does define what happened *to me.*

TOTALLY NUMB

My wife was seriously ill and I loved her very much. We had been involved in a serious car crash, and the doctor didn't expect her to survive the night. (Shirley survived, but that's another story.)

As I sat by her bedside in the hospital and stared at her pain-streaked face, I felt nothing. *I was totally numb.* What's wrong with me? I asked myself. This is the person I love most and I can't feel anything.

That wasn't the first time I had numbed out; it wasn't the last time. Over the years, I encountered extremely difficult situations and yet felt nothing. I was sure that something was defective in me. To make it worse, occasionally I cried, but it was always about someone with whom I had no strong emotional ties. I didn't understand how I could be sad over small things and yet feel nothing about the hurt of those I loved most.

Here's how I finally understood what happened. While I was doing my usual predawn run, a car made a U-turn in front of me and knocked me down. I felt no pain, but three days later I sensed what I called a little discomfort in my left hip. It didn't hurt, but it was a nuisance. A week later, and at my wife's urging, I went to a chiropractor and he did a number of tests.

He kept asking, "Does this hurt?" He kept probing, but nothing he did caused me to say yes. "You have a very high tolerance for pain," he finally said.

On the phone a few days later, I related that incident to my younger brother Chuck. He laughed and said, "Don't you remember how Dad beat us and we didn't cry? *We didn't feel it.*"

Just then the numbness made sense. Whenever powerful emotions overwhelmed me, I numbed out. Because I couldn't cope with the crushing impact, I had no feelings. Every day for weeks, I prayed, "Lord, help me feel my emotions. Let me experience anguish and pain."

Slowly I began to feel. I've since learned to reclaim my emotions. To some it may sound strange, but I've learned to praise God because I felt sad when my wife hurts or one of my children has a serious problem. Or when pain strikes my body.

Lord, remind me that I no longer need to numb out.
It's all right to hurt and I want to feel my emotions.

INNOCENCE LOST

I used to wonder why victims of molestation assumed responsibility for the damage done to them by sexual abuse. I was one of those who felt culpable even though I had no control over my childhood being decimated.

Through the stories I know of other men who have been molested in childhood, I've realized we have that in common: we all feel guilty. We're unable to reason out that the wrong was done to us, not that we were wrong. The guilt seems to come from realizing we suddenly know too much. The guilt that I accepted kept me from talking to anyone, or realizing that there were possibly safe adults I could talk to.

One thing that helped me overcome my sense of guilt was to realize that I wasn't the one who was tempted to do something that went against the laws of nature or God. Something abusive was done *to* me. By realizing that truth in my journey of seeking healing from the damage of the abuse done to me in those early twelve years, it's easier and easier to believe that it wasn't my fault and there was nothing I could have done differently.

A powerful moment of insight occurred back in 1994, when I first visited my father's grave. As I wept and spoke words of forgiveness and healing (for my benefit), I had a new ache in my heart considering the pain he had probably endured in his life, pain that very well could have originated from his own loss of innocence.

I've also considered how my own abuse isn't an excuse for actions that I've taken because of my own brokenness and need for healing. At times, I responded out of my own pain and have hurt those I love the most. But I'm learning.

Because of my lost innocence, healing and restoration come from accepting the truth that all of us are wounded. The pain in our lives is that we lost our innocence, whether given or taken away. If people can still love *me* in spite of that, who am I to withhold love, grace, and forgiveness when I've been wronged?

In that knowledge and strength, I find my own innocence being restored because I extend grace to others.

> God, help me love and nurture the little boy
> who was molested. Help me extend that
> quality of love to anyone who hurts.

UTTERLY WORTHLESS

"A strong component of childhood sexual molestation becomes a systematic tearing down of boys and interferes with their development." I don't know where I read this, but a few years ago I copied these words in a notebook. Another statement in my notes reads, "Abuse assaults the boy's self-understanding and makes him feel unworthy of love and affection."[1] This statement referred to emotional abuse but it applies to sexual abuse as well.

Those two quotations nicely expressed my self-concept. I felt unworthy of love and affection. That's such a terrible burden to impose on a young boy who's trying to navigate the murky rivers of life.

Unworthy. I don't know that I ever used that particular word, but it sums up my childhood. Unworthy of love. Unworthy of being accepted. Because I had no one to whom I could confide, it meant I had to face those struggles on my own. No wonder I always felt different and unlike other boys.

✦　✦　✦

One thing I had to face is that we don't "just get healed" or grow up healthy. It's work—hard work. We survivors start at a distinct disadvantage unless we have a strong support system. We need other people and perhaps we know it—we just don't know how to ask for or receive their help.

Looking back, I'm sure there were adults to whom I might have entrusted my secrets, but I didn't know how to talk about my feeling different. Most of all, however, I honestly didn't think anyone cared. That's the damaged self-image.

When I was twelve or thirteen years old, my life hit such a low point I decided to commit suicide by jabbing myself repeatedly in the stomach with a knife. (I'd seen it done that way in a movie.) At the last minute, however, I couldn't do it. I cursed myself for being a coward.

When our self-esteem is so skewed and twisted, *we blame ourselves* for everything, even when we're unable to complete the most self-destructive urges. Taking my own life seemed to be the only sensible solution.

Looking back, I can't pick an aha moment when my life changed. For me, it was a gradual movement. I credit most of that growth to the love and patience of my late wife, Shirley, who refused to give up on me.

It comes down to this. If you want healing from your childhood abuse, face one harsh reality: *You can't do it yourself. You can't heal without the loving, accepting help of others.*

God, I don't want to feel worthless. Heal me, loving God.

DEFINING MYSELF

"It was all a lie," Max, a twenty-three-year-old, said to me. He told me about the leader in his church who befriended him when he was in his early teens.

"I was the only boy who didn't like sports, and my classmates called me 'faggot,' even though I didn't know what the word meant until later.

"The youth leader encouraged me. 'You're a nice, sweet kid. Don't pay attention to what they're saying.' He spent time with me and he was the first adult who ever listened to me. After I cried, he hugged me and whispered, 'It's all right to cry. Let it go.'

"After that, we started with hugs and I felt so grateful to have a friend. I didn't like it when he taught me to masturbate him and the other things, but I loved the man so much I would have done anything for him. 'It's our secret,' he said. 'Just you and me.'

"I thought he really loved me. The church fired him, and he refused to talk with me. So it was all lies. He hurt me, and I thought he truly loved me."

Max and I met at the 2016 annual conference of Hope for Wholeness.[2] "For a couple of years, I became that faggot my classmates labeled me," he said.

When Max was twenty years old, he was not only a survivor of abuse, but also a miserable drug addict, college dropout, and isolated from his parents. He attempted to take his own life and obviously didn't succeed. A wise therapist suggested that he attend the Hope for Wholeness conference.

That was three years before we met, and he said that group saved his life.

"My classmates were wrong about me," he said. "And for the first time in my life, I'm happy and like who I am."

"I can define myself," Max said. "I don't give anyone else that privilege."

> God, you can define me; you can teach me to
> define myself. But only you and I can do that.
> Please help me to define myself as you do.

— *12* —

SOMETIMES I THINK I'M CRAZY

I've heard that statement from survivors several times, and I assume it's fairly common. They don't usually mean they think they're insane, but rather that their lives don't make sense. They're confused about values and behavior.

That doesn't make them crazy, even though they may feel that way. They speak of conflicting emotions and often of not trusting their perceptions.

Why wouldn't we feel strange or odd? When we tried to tell the truth, we weren't believed. Or we were told we were wrong when we spoke up.

In my home truth was constantly twisted, even in minor things. For example, I remember quite clearly I once said to my mother, "You like Mel more than you like me." Mel was one of my younger brothers.

"I love all of you the same," she said.

As young as I was, that statement didn't make sense to me. I *knew* Mel was the favorite. Years later, my other siblings and I talked about my younger brother, and we all agreed he was the favorite.

Because I wasn't believed when I made a simple observation, why would I expect my parents to believe me on something like sexual assault?

We're not crazy; we're hurting or confused, but if we persist in seeking answers and God's healing, life will make sense.

Loving God, thank you for helping me make sense of my life.

WILL IT EVER END?

I asked that question a few months into what we now call my recovery period. The pain was intense. In some ways, I felt victimized a second time. "I had to go through that as a kid," I said to my wife. "Now that I understand what was going on, it hurts even worse."

Maybe it wasn't worse; maybe it only felt worse.

And the pain went on a long time. I didn't keep any record, but the most intense period was probably for about two years. I had opened the door and I couldn't shut it. I knew I had to keep going.

I've long moved past the worst pain. The memories have begun to dull the way most memories do. That's one powerful reward for pushing forward.

But there's more.

These days I enjoy healthier, deeper, and more honest relationships than ever. I like being who I am and look forward to who I'm becoming. You might still be in the throes of the worst pain, but it will get better. Bit by bit.

> Loving God, remind me, even in the midst
> of pain, the journey is worth it.

LIES I BELIEVED
Dann Youle

Like most kids from abusive homes, there were many lies I believed were absolutely true.

I believed that somewhere there really was a "perfect" family. *Ozzie and Harriet, Leave It to Beaver,* and *The Andy Griffith Show* perpetuated it as well. Even though there were no alcoholics in my family of origin, and even though abuse didn't happen overtly in my family, I knew we didn't have the perfect family.

But the *big* lie I believed was that I would *never* be a man. I was always the "good boy," but even that wasn't good enough. Having been abused sexually and discarded by my grandpa, struggling with same-sex attraction, not receiving the love and affirmation from my father the way I needed, I realize that at age forty-five I *still* don't always feel like I'm a man!

I know I am a man—a real man—and I'm learning to define myself the way that God sees me. The American ideal of a man I'm not, and I'm finally learning that that's okay. I don't need to achieve the *Ozzie and Harriet* portrayal of a perfect family either, and that too is okay.

For the longest time, I couldn't move forward in life because I felt like I didn't have what it takes to have real "masculine initiative" and do the things I know I'm called to do. I'm still learning and have a *long* way to go, but at least I've started back to school, and I know I can accomplish all God has for me.

It's a great feeling: I'm truly the man God has called me to be and I am increasingly becoming more and more that man.

God, thank you that I no longer need to believe
lies about myself. Please continue leading
me into truth and understanding.

— *15* —

THE WAY TO HEAL

After I went public about my abusive childhood, many people reached out to me—and I appreciated their concern and compassion. A few of them, however, weren't helpful. I call them the right-way-to-heal people. They knew all the rules and emotions associated with grief and (even more important) knew exactly what I needed to do for myself.

Most of their advice came from their own experiences. Not only did I understand, I appreciated their willingness to share their pain and healing with me.

What they didn't seem to grasp was that I wasn't like them—and no one else is either. What worked for them might not work for someone else. As obvious as that may be, too many of them had become the right-way-to-heal people.

Here are examples of the advice I received.

- "Talk about it. Tell anyone who'll listen. The more you speak about it, the easier it gets."
- "Be extremely selective about whom you tell. You don't want to cast pearls before swine."
- "You need a therapist. They're the only ones who can help you."
- "Don't go to a professional. Find a friend or a small group—individuals who have recovered from abuse. They're the ones who can help."

No wonder I was confused.

✦ ✦ ✦

Many recovering survivors helped me by sharing their stories. Within a few months after I began my recovery, I attended a men's conference and one small group (or break-out session as we call them today) focused on

33

men who were abused in childhood. With great trepidation, I joined six other men. And that one-hour session was exactly what I needed.

They were the first survivors I'd ever openly talked to about my childhood. Until then, *emotionally* I felt as if I were struggling alone in a vast ocean and the current was trying to pull me under.

Sometimes I think healing from childhood molestation is much like grief recovery. And it really is. For instance, during the weeks after Shirley's death I received fifteen books on dealing with loss. I deeply appreciate those who took time to send me tools they felt would help. And I read at least parts of all of them.

I had previously experienced grief—the death of my son-in-law, both of my parents, my three brothers, and a number of close friends. I mention that only because some of the *commands* (and that's how they came across) set up rules. Not that they wouldn't have been good suggestions, but it was the spirit in which they came.

"Make no serious decisions for at least a year." Generally, I agreed with that, but I hated to see it put down as some kind of must-follow commandment.

"You need to give yourself three years to get beyond your grief," one woman stressed and then added, "That's how long it took me." That second statement told me about how she grieved. And *for her*, that was the right way to process her loss.

For at least two years I had faced the reality that Shirley was dying—and I began a kind of pre-grieving for me. About four months after Shirley died, I tried to explain my emotions to someone. "I miss Shirley, and I wish she were still here, but I'm handling this fairly well. And when I start grieving, I say three words aloud: 'No more pain.'"

That right-way-to-grieve person insisted I was denying my grief and would one day fall apart with grief. It seemed not to have occurred to my friend that we grieve differently.

Lord, help me listen to others, and be
sensitive to their healing journey.

IF IT FELT GOOD, DOES THAT MEAN I'M GAY?

This is the question most men *don't* ask aloud. I want to mention that it's natural for sexual abuse to feel good. When someone stimulates our sexual organs, an erection is a natural phenomenon. Tyler Perry, speaking of his abuse during an Oprah Winfrey program about sexual abuse, said, "I felt my body betraying me."[3] I'd say, "No, your body reacted in a normal, natural manner."

But the fact that our bodies reacted normally doesn't always relieve our minds. One abuse survivor has only one wife but nine children. "If anyone tried to call me gay," he said, "I could point to my kids and prove them wrong." Then, with tear-filled eyes he asked, "So why do I wonder if I am gay?"

This is a common concern of those who have been sexually abused. Some men become sexually compulsive with women—which I see as part of their unresolved issues. That's a way of shouting, "See! I'm not gay!"

An oft-held belief today is that gender identity is established around age two or three.[4] And there seems to be no research to prove that being victimized makes the survivor a homosexual. So just because you were abused and it felt good, doesn't mean you're gay.

Most of the abused men I've met are, in fact, heterosexual. My guess is that the current thinking is probably right about the formation of sexual identity—our natural inclinations are set at an early age.

> God, help me overcome everything that once defined me
> as a victim. Remind me that I'm a survivor. And more.

— *17* —

BUT IT FELT GOOD

I don't know how many men I've talked with who equated abuse with excitement. It felt good, and consequently they questioned their own sexuality and whether they did something to make it happen.

We need to admit that when we were sexually assaulted it felt good. Of course it did.

I still recall the old man running his hands around my body telling me how soft it felt and I enjoyed his touch. All of us have skin hunger and no one in my family ever touched me—or if so, I don't remember.

Everything the old man did to me felt good. In retrospect, I felt shame for responding to a natural, normal act—the human touch.

An online article stated that three of four adults agree with the statement, "Americans suffer from skin hunger,"[5] or an unmet natural desire for human touch. I don't know how those numbers were determined, but I accept it. Our perpetrators used that unfulfilled human need and we suffered because of it.

> Heavenly Father, I was an innocent boy who needed loving
> touches; my perpetrator exploited a basic human need.
> Remind me of that innocence as you continue to heal me.

IT HAPPENED ONLY ONCE

Abuse is abuse, regardless of the number of times or whether it was sexual, a physical beating, or verbal and emotional hammering.

It happened.

It's not how many times it happened, but the real question should be this: How did it affect the boy who was abused?

If he was traumatized, and it happened only one time, that's still once. That's like saying, "The robber stole my money. It happened only once, so was I robbed?"

One time. Thirty times. Forget counting. *How did it affect you?* What damage did it do to your childhood? What havoc did the abuse create in your life?

> Lord, remind me that the number of times I was
> abused means little; how the abuse affected all
> the areas of my life is what matters. And I depend
> on you to free me—once and always.

INVISIBLE
Tom Scales

"Dear Lord, I pray that today you will make me invisible."

Growing up in a world of childhood sexual abuse, I was preoccupied with being so invisible that I never attracted attention. It was a challenging path. I wanted to fit in with others and be part of groups and teams; I wanted to have friends. Yet I wanted to keep my inner self hidden.

I dreaded others finding out. I feared that my distorted sense of right and wrong would surface in embarrassing ways.

I mentally wrote scripts for conversations to avoid the risks of vulnerability that openness and honesty could bring. I analyzed and planned everything I could.

Silence and isolation became my friends. They offered safety with no judgment. Over time, they helped me to build strong and impenetrable walls. As an adult, I couldn't afford the vulnerability of youth because the stakes of job and family are higher. The longer I held the secret, the more powerfully I feared exposure. As a result, I sacrificed joy, friendship, intimacy, and other life-fulfilling pleasures to fortify those walls.

All-powerful God, thank you for seeing the real me.
Help me to become visible and open to others.

LOGIC VERSUS EMOTION

I once mentioned in a keynote address at a conference that I had been sexually molested. I didn't dwell on the issue, but said it affected the way I perceived life.

Afterward a man who identified himself as a pastor-therapist said to me, "You didn't do anything to cause the assault. It was your perpetrator's fault."

I tried to tell him that I knew, but he didn't seem to hear me. He talked for another minute or two, but his words and attitude seemed to say to me, "I've explained the logic of the situation and now you're free."

I agreed with his reasoning. I had been a child, and of course I didn't do anything to bring on the molestation. It was the fault of my perpetrators. If acknowledging the truth were all I needed, I would have been free much earlier.

Despite my few protests, he couldn't seem to grasp that my *emotions* hadn't caught up with my cognitive perceptions. I could make the same statements he made—and I did—but they hadn't set me free. It was a long time before I could *feel* free.

And, sad to say, some men never feel fault-free.

God of all emotions, set me free. Remind me that you created
me, love me, and want to set me free from emotional pain.

THE WHY QUESTIONS

Many of the emails that come to my personal box ask why in some form.

Here's my answer: I don't know. I'm not sure anyone can fully give the reasons behind the queries about pain, injustice, healing, and anguish.

But is that the question we really need answered?

Instead of asking for the reason something happens, it's more healthful to focus on the deeper, perhaps unasked questions.

Here's my major reason for suggesting this: when we ask why, the natural answer is logical and analytical. Suppose the Holy Spirit whispered to us, giving us three reasons or five.

So what? We may gain information, but the problem still remains. Logical answers don't satisfy emotional needs, no matter how fervently we ask.

We rarely find help because our issues come from multilayered pain and we want satisfying emotional responses.

Instead of pushing the why button, a better approach is to ask, "What do I need?" "How do I receive healing?"

When I've mentioned this a few times to people who push the why question, I listen and try to intuit what I think is the underlying question. For example, I might say, "I wonder if your real issue is that you want to feel loved."

Even if I'm not quite on target—and a few times I haven't been—it encourages them to reflect and decide what they really want.

> Lord, I know it's not wrong to ask, "Why?" But
> I know it's wiser to ask, "What do I need?" Give
> me wisdom to ask the right questions.

WHY? WHY? WHY?

In his book *Heartbroken*, my friend Gary Roe writes: "'Why?' often has no answers; yet our wounded hearts must still ask the question."[6] His book isn't about sexual assault, but the quote is still powerful.

Almost all of us ask that question at some point. Reasons aren't what we truly want; we want comfort and we want to make sense of things. It's not logical that an adult would rape a child. But it happens, and we're the survivors who often can't figure it out.

Too often we blame ourselves with sentences that begin, "If only I had . . ." or "If only I hadn't . . ." We want to believe we live in a rational world with explanations for everything.

Sometimes there are no explanations, only facts.

I don't know the reason I was victimized; I do know I don't want to live my life as a victim.

Instead I ask, "How do I continue to heal?" And for this question, there are answers.

> All-wise God, you know all the answers, even
> to the questions I can't articulate. You know
> my heart. Thank you for loving me.

WHAT DOES IT MEAN TO BE A MAN?

That's a frequent question from men who were sexually molested in childhood. What does it mean to be a man—a real man?

We have cultural attitudes and expectations about masculinity within our own social communities. But no matter how it's said, most of us survivors face uncertainty about our manhood. Many of us feel challenged and unsure. We say to ourselves, "If I were a real man, I would (or I wouldn't) . . ."

For example, we think, *Because I was a victim of sexual abuse, I can't be a real man. True men are never victims.* If I think of the word *victim* when I think of myself, I may struggle or be aware of something others say that makes me feel I don't measure up to society's standards.

If I cry, my friends may laugh at me, imply that I'm a sissy or I behave like a girl. I wasn't athletic, and I've never enjoyed watching football. Or perhaps I feel I'm too thin or too fat—almost anything can cause me to struggle with deeper issues.

It's sad, but too often, like other men, I fought a silent inner battle. For most of my life, I couldn't share my shame and self-disgust. To do that only made me feel more open to further criticism.

Years ago, my friend Charlie said he played with paper dolls. He was an only child and the dolls entertained him. One day he was with a friend and they saw two girls playing with paper dolls. "Only girls play with real dolls or paper dolls," his friend said dismissively.

After that, Charlie said, "I played only in my room and made sure no one else would find them." He later said that he started dating girls at age sixteen, and even though he liked girls, later married, and was never involved in any homosexual relationships, he still wonders if he's really a man.

> Caring God, help me admit that I *am* a real man. I don't have
> to follow the macho behavior. Help me know that being a
> true man is an inside job, not based on others' standards.

MY INNER CIRCLE

"I have an inner circle—myself."

Of all the things the man said, that's all I remember. It took place in a meeting where I was the guest speaker, and several people responded to various questions about being open with a few people. I had suggested they establish an inner circle—a cadre of people they could trust, such as two or three individuals.

The man admitted that he had never had a close friend, and "I used sex as a way to achieve love." He added, "For a few minutes I felt good, but afterward I felt worse.

"I can't open up to anyone because I'm afraid they'll tell somebody or become disgusted with me."

Before I had a chance to respond, the leader of the group said to him, "Several of us felt that way when we first came."

"Yeah, I was one of them," another man called out. "But after three meetings here, I learned that some of their junk was worse than mine."

Another man called out, "One day I opened up and told the group a couple of terrible things I had done and assumed they'd tell me not to come back. No one seemed shocked." He smiled before he added, "It's still not easy, but the only way I know to get rid of those fears and inner demons is to tell someone else. And these guys have pulled me out of my self-disgust."

I could have said many things that evening in response to the man's confession about isolation, but the other twenty-plus men did a splendid job. The next thing I remember saying is, "When you admitted to us about being isolated from everyone else, you were trusting us. We could have told you what a jerk you were, but none did."

His eyes clouded up, he nodded, and dropped his head into his hands.

One man walked across the room, hugged the newcomer, and said, "I want to be your friend."

I don't know the end of that story, but I sensed two things. First, the newcomer opened himself—not a lot, but enough to admit his aloneness. Second, the others nodded, encouraged him, and one of them embraced him.

The healing had begun.

> Lord, we all need an inner circle. Help me open up to others so you can use them as healing instruments.

BEING IGNORED

As a child, I was beaten by my father, sexually assaulted by a female relative, and verbally abused by both parents. The worst part of my childhood, or so it seems to me now, was being ignored.

Years later, my late sister Evelyn said, "You were a quiet kid and most of the time we didn't seem to know you were around."

Mel was two years younger and died from alcohol abuse at age forty-eight, but he was clearly my parents' favorite child and we other six siblings knew and accepted it. In my parents' eyes, Mel did no wrong. Ever. When he got into trouble—with regularity—they didn't punish or rebuke him.

I envied Mel and wished my parents cared for me like that. He received the praise and I was ignored. I've tried to think of one rule my parents gave me, such as when to go to bed at night or get up in the morning, what subjects to take in school, or restrictions about behavior or friends. None. I learned to make all those decisions on my own. As a boy, I decided to be in bed at night by nine while Mel sometimes stayed up until midnight (and was regularly "too sick" to go to school the next day).

The time I contemplated suicide I did think about being missed. I distinctly recall thinking, my mother will cry a little, but within days everyone will have forgotten me. I truly believed that.

Perhaps because I was the good boy—the one who didn't get into trouble, did well in school, and didn't demand attention—they found it easy to ignore me.

I didn't ask for attention, probably because I didn't think it would do any good. That reality helps me understand why I was such a prime target for a pedophile. Whenever anyone showed me attention or interest, they had me. I was a ready-to-be-victimized child.

That was a long time ago, but those memories aren't gone. I don't need to be the center of attention, but I do have a huge need to be cared about and loved.

Like any normal person.

I'm grateful for those special people in my life who expressed genuine love and affection for me. They (with God's guidance) helped me to become who I am today.

God, thank you for the truly special people in
my life who loved me. They helped make me
who I am today and who I'm becoming.

TRUST
Roger Mann

Trust has always been a huge issue for me. My father was very strict, very harsh at times, and I would become self-protective. Then at night he would sneak into my room and be so touching and caressing. I opened up and welcomed his advances like the starving child I was, only to find him distant and angry again the next day.

It became such a part of my life not to trust that I didn't even notice it until others began to tell me of how they dealt with it in their lives. It was like, *Oh man, I do that too!* For instance, I would walk into any room and gravitate immediately toward the corner or a seat facing the door, back to the wall. Until a friend spoke about his realizing why he was doing it, I was totally unconscious of it myself.

Or the matter of personal space—being stopped in a hallway to chat and putting my back to the wall. And a thousand other odd things like assuming when someone said they wanted to speak to me it meant something bad. Assuming all compliments were preemptive for someone wanting something.

At the same time, being so gullible that when a compliment seemed to be sincere, I would fall for some kind of rip-off scheme because I desperately wanted to believe this person liked me. I know that sounds paradoxical but there was always this waiting for the other shoe to drop and yet wanting desperately to believe this time it would be different.

I was so untrusting, yet desperately wanting to trust, needing to believe I was worthy of another's kindness and becoming an easy mark. I suspended rational thought because of that need and fear of trusting. That was an area of my life that was invisible to me until I talked with other survivors. Our stories are different, but our wounds are familiar.

Loving God, I want to trust you. I want to trust
others, but I need your help. Teach me to trust.

WHERE TRUST STARTS

When I felt safe, I was ready to face the pain of the past. But part of that sense of safety stayed at bay until I was able to trust myself—to believe I was worthwhile and trustworthy.

I've frequently written about trusting others, and that's a big issue for most of us. I've discovered that trust issues have to start with ourselves. Until I sensed I was loved, truly loved, I felt worthless and driven to prove my value to others, but especially *to myself*. I didn't know how to trust my own judgment. That meant I didn't know how to trust myself.

Healing begins as an inside job. My wife and others expressed their acceptance and affection for years, and yet deep inside, I felt they were conditional: as long as I met their standards for my behavior, I was all right. But one day I believed their unconditional love, and healing began.

Once we're able to accept ourselves and feel some level of self-compassion, we can accept the self-affirmations and care from others.

Trust does begin within, but knowing we're loved by others sets up the ability to believe in ourselves.

God, help me to see myself as you do. Help
me to trust myself and see my value.

TRUSTING OTHERS
Tom Scales

For victims of childhood sexual abuse, the most damaging and persistent negative impact for most is the inability to trust. Certainly, there are many results of self-destruction. Without question, our boundaries are distorted, but trust is at the foundation of our personality and our relations.

As I grew into adulthood, I trusted absolutely no one. I had friends, but my friends never had me. At no time did I feel comfortable enough to be vulnerable or allow another person into the emotional cave where I hid. God brought some very special people into my life so that this could change.

Some of those people were in the support group at Johnson Ferry Baptist Church in Marietta, Georgia. It was there that I truly understood I was not alone. I heard the tragic stories of other men and women and realized that it made no difference if it was a man or a woman, if the abuse happened one time or thousands over years, the damage was much the same.

In that group, we showed each other the true meaning of trust and what it looks like in real life. We talked openly about struggles, fears, and our path so far. We found that each, in a different way, had been programmed by the predators, and those around us who turned a blind eye, to see the worst, expect the worst, and not accept joy, affection, love, or appreciation, because we were clearly unworthy and undeserving.

We talked about the negative tapes that played over and over in our minds, triggered often by a voice, a smell, a word, or a tone of voice. We were quickly back in the body of the abused little boy or girl, searching for the mental and emotional hiding place where we lived as kids. We learned to replace those tapes with the love, affection, and trust we shared in that group.

The discussions were the foundation for learning to properly build trust. It started with introspection of our own personal boundaries. Having been sexually molested by at least eight different men and held down and raped by a young woman before I was thirteen helped create a boundary system where just about anything was not only okay but encouraged.

As I grew up, I knew my thinking and my emotions were distorted and as a result I replaced them with huge, solid walls. They kept everyone and all emotions out. That didn't work very well either.

Over the last few years, as I have rebuilt those boundaries, I have learned to allow in love, openness, vulnerability, friendship, and affection, without evil distortion. I have learned that no one crosses those boundaries without permission, not even me. Once I had appropriate boundaries in place, trust became easier. I understood where I started and stopped and where others began (emotionally, physically, spiritually) and I appreciated the significance of that separation.

I also learned that I needed to recheck relationships and behaviors from time to time to be sure that the boundaries were not creeping or behaviors edging across the line.

The path from victim to victor is a lifelong journey and each positive step is a cause for joy and celebration in itself.

> God, I had friends, but my friends never had me.
> Please teach me to trust others.

ONLY MY IMAGINATION

"How do I know the memories and flashbacks are real?" one man said. "I've always had a good imagination."

My answer: *you know the difference.* The question isn't, "Are they real?" but "Can I accept them?" When the memories first started pouring into my heart and mind, I, like many others, didn't want to believe them as being authentic. *But I knew.*

No matter how hard I tried I couldn't convince myself that I had made them up. *I knew.*

I didn't have a lot of flashbacks—where childhood memories forced themselves into my head. What I had most were dreams—nightmares— and I awakened in a sweat and sometimes shaking. Those dreams were quite literal, as opposed to what I call the hamburger-and-onion type—the kind that troubles me over something I ate.

In the dreams, I was a child again and I relived most of the tormenting, painful abuse.

Particularly, I remember the old man who rented a room from us. In the nightmares, he was ugly and I was afraid, but I went up to him anyway. When I was awake, I thought of him as having a kind face and he often smiled.

In my dreams, I especially remembered his male-pattern baldness with no hair except on the sides of his face. Unless he went outside, he wore sleeveless undershirts and tufts of white, curly hair showed over the top of the shirt.

I mention the hair because he knelt down (or in some dreams he put me on his lap) and asked me to feel his hairy chest. My dreams never went beyond that but I knew they didn't go there because I couldn't face what followed.

Dream after dream came to me over a period of months. Each time I awakened abruptly, feeling frightened, and sometimes couldn't go back to sleep.

Once I learned to accept the reality of those scenes, they went away. I don't need them because I faced the pain, betrayal, and mourned the loss of my childhood.

Through the help of God and my friends, I've stayed on the healing path. I'm closer to the end of the recovery road. Until then, I have to say, "I'm not quite healed. But close."

Loving God, free me from flashbacks and dreams.
Help me put them behind me forever.

— *30* —

FANTASY

I wonder how many of us had a rich fantasy life. I never thought much about that until recently. I had a vivid imagination and put myself in every kind of troubled, problematic situation and always, always came out victorious.

As a child that fantasizing probably "saved" my life. I learned to pretend, to imagine a happy life where everything was fine. During intense periods of pain, I discovered solace in my pretend world. In school, I was skinny. Short. Not athletic. One of the two or three kids the captains argued over. "You take him this time. I got stuck with him the last time."

My late friend Steve Grubmann told me that he invented an imaginary friend who was there for him in those painful times. That was how he coped.

As I thought about fantasy, I remembered the verses from the famous love chapter of 1 Corinthians. The apostle Paul said that when he was a child he thought and behaved as a child, but after he became an adult, he pushed those things out of his mind (see 13:11).

Many of us received temporary peace through our imagination or pretense. And we can look back and be thankful that we could face some of our problems, even if they were only in our imagination. Like Steve, many of us received temporary peace through our imaginations. As adults, we can learn to face our problems realistically. This is moving beyond our pain and living outside the world of our abused childhood.

I still have fantasies, but I've noticed in the last ten years they're far more benign and rather fun. I focus on events or experiences when I relive a situation and think of what I might have said to make me smug. But I don't need them any more to escape an impoverished, stolen childhood.

Lord, help me live in reality; free me from my fantasies.

DENIAL—A SURVIVAL TOOL

In my book, *When a Man You Love Was Abused,* I wrote about my amnesia (which is a form of denial). After reading it, one man wrote, "Denial was a powerful survival tool for me when I was a boy. Now I'm an adult and I struggle to be free. Now I wish I could forget but I know I need to face it."

I understand his situation. Denial worked for us when we needed it to endure life. As I think over my own life, I'm convinced my denial helped me cope as well as I did. We had few resources and were innocent and naive about life.

Here's how I think about amnesia for us survivors: In first grade I learned to count by using my fingers. I haven't had to count that way since I was a child. The method worked until I was mature enough to leave a beginner's method behind.

As adults, we're more sophisticated and can reason out the issues. Most of all, we can step back and look at our feelings, analyzing them with insight that only comes with maturity. The pain was intense when I began recovery, but I reminded myself that I truly felt the pain. My amnesia had taught me to deny my deepest feelings; my healing liberates my feelings.

> God, sometimes I feel the hurt, but it reminds me
> that my emotions are working and that I'm no
> longer living in denial. Thank you for feelings.

A MATTER OF TIMING

Some believe that the younger a child was when the abuse occurred or the wider the age difference between the victim and the perpetrator, the worse the impact will be on him or her as a survivor. But I haven't seen any evidence to back up this theory. Another theory is that the more deviant the perpetrator's behavior, the more damaging it is to the survivor's recovery and the deeper the issues he or she must work through as an adult. Again, I haven't seen any evidence of this.

Although I'm no expert who can disprove these ideas, both ignore the personality of the child.

We all heal differently. Some boys are more sensitive than others; some survivors never seem to overcome the effects.

Immediately I think of John, a member of a small group of six men I joined during the initial year of my coming to terms with my abuse.

In one of our first meetings, John told us about his painful childhood of abuse and it sounded much like mine, except his was a single perpetrator. He had been seeing a therapist for twenty years. He ended by saying, "I feel like a bag of manure."

Our group met every Thursday and I remained with them four years, until I moved out of the city. At the last meeting, John made the same statement about himself.

I haven't seen John since, but I wonder how he feels about himself today. My guess is that he's probably at about the same level as he was back when he was part of the group.

Why was John unable to recover after more than two decades of therapy? I don't know. I'm hesitant to say it was because his abuse took place so early. Or blame the length of it. I could say the same things about mine. John knew his abuser was at least twenty-five years older. The old man who assaulted me was more than sixty years older than I was and the woman was thirty-seven years older.

Why have I been able to achieve almost-but-not-quite healed status and John seemed stuck? I don't know.

I'm grateful for the friends and loved ones who have stood with me and helped me. I'm even more grateful to a benevolent and compassionate God.

Why me? Why have I moved so far down that road?

I have no idea, but I do know that comparing my recovery to someone else's does me no good. Instead, I focus on the progress I've made and am filled with gratitude for whatever growth I see there.

Healing God, I don't understand why every man isn't healed,
but I'm grateful your healing hand has been on me.
Thank you.

TRIGGERS
Tom Scales

What we call triggers remind me of my past. Something happens that throws me back to my painful abuse. It can be a voice, a smell, an event, a person, or a place that thrusts me back to the sensations and world of sexual abuse. As an adult, when I experienced a trigger that reminded me of my past, my old companions of silence and isolation protected me once again. I built an unbreachable wall and refused to let anything inside—even those things that could heal me.

The break from those devastating triggers came while listening to a TV interview with Frank Fitzpatrick, who was being interviewed about the sexual abuse he suffered at the hands of Father James Porter.

In that moment, it was as if someone had flipped the switch and a torrent of ugly memories flooded in. At times they were overwhelming and seemed never to stop, as the actions of one predator after another paraded themselves through my consciousness.

I could no longer ignore what had happened to me. Though painful, the tidal wave of memories sent me on a journey outside my walls to find healing. That TV interview and the many steps and events that followed brought me out of my emotional cave. By recognizing those triggers, I've been able to overcome the impervious walls with appropriate physical, emotional, and spiritual boundaries.

The process strengthened my faith and my self-esteem. It allowed me to have true friends and to experience joy. I was able to cast off the persistent depression that had stayed with me throughout my life.

Transformation from being a silent, isolated victim to becoming an emotionally healthy individual is possible for all survivors. For me, a TV interview was the start. I'd like to be part of the starting experience for others.

Thank you, omnipotent God, that not only is
transformation possible but you have made it a reality.

A GOOD FEAR

For a long time, Ryan worried that he would turn around and abuse boys the way he had been abused. He didn't know if that was a rational fear or not, but he knew the thought tormented him. *What if I ended up hurting a boy or many boys the way I had been hurt?*

He said of his fear, "After I married, we had two girls and that didn't seem to be any problem and our third was a boy. That almost freaked me out. I told my wife about my fear, which I'd never done before."

"As long as you're afraid of doing it, I think you'll be fine," she said. "That fear holds you back."

Ryan said at the end of his email to me, "Maybe that sounds too simplistic, but it did so much for me. Our son is now ten and I've never hurt him. Sometimes fear is good."

Loving God, help me move forward in my healing. Strengthen
me so I'll never have to fear that I'll become an abuser.

YOU DON'T NEED TO FEEL ASHAMED

Some statements irritate me. "You don't need to feel guilty," or "You have no reason to feel ashamed" are two of them. I wonder about the people who say those things. How can they speak so glibly?

Of course, we need to feel ashamed or guilty—it's a natural reaction to what happened to us. No one explained to us that something bad was done to us. Consequently, we felt those negative emotions. We weren't mature enough to grasp that we were innocent, so shame and guilt invaded our souls.

People don't seem to realize that if I could have freed myself from those two emotions, I would have done it long ago. Instead it took me many, many years before I felt the freedom from those enslavements.

I don't think I'm unusual.

I'd like to say to those glib-speaking individuals, "Don't tell anyone how he should or shouldn't feel. That advice helps no one."

Instead, I wish they would say something simple such as, "I'm sorry you're hurting."

> God of grace, free me from feelings of shame and guilt. You're
> the only one who can rightfully say, "Don't feel that way."

THE BLAME GAME

Ron called it the family blame game.

"In our family, we had to find out who was wrong and then we could move on," Ron said and pointed out that the blame game had been ingrained in him and his siblings. He dated Darlene (who became his wife), and "during her first visit to my family, she saw that game in action. All the screaming, lecturing, and finger pointing happened because someone had left an empty glass on a wooden table."

"I was stunned," Ron said, "because I hadn't realized what we did to each other until I saw the family through Darlene's eyes."

"It was like a criminal investigation you might see on TV," Darlene commented after they left the house. "Does it make any difference who did it? The effect is the same."

Those words forced Ron to think about his life and particularly the molestation he went through. "It hit me: I blamed my uncle who abused me." Finally, Ron stopped focusing on blaming and turned his attention to the effect. The problems were the same, no matter who perpetrated them.

"It sounds like a small thing to many," he said, "but as long as I played the blame game, I focused my anger on *who* did it instead of *what* he did. And it wasn't just abuse—it was anything that went wrong."

The blame game diverts our attention so that we don't try to cope with the results. And it's the consequences that need examining. That doesn't absolve the culprit, and forgiving him is another issue to face.

Ron, like others, spent so much effort in pointing to the guilty, he had no insight into what had happened to him.

Isn't that the way it sometimes works in our lives? We charge the wrongdoer and don't move on to ask, "But what has this done to me?"

> Forgiving God, remind me that you have a better
> way. Instead of blaming, help me to forgive.

IT'S SO HARD

About six months after I first dealt with my sexual assault, I had made progress, but the process seemed to go on and on. "Why is it so hard?" I asked Steve Grubmann, a fellow survivor.

"The deeper the wound, the slower the healing." Those aren't Steve's exact words, but I knew what he meant. We were naive, innocent kids and they turned our world upside down.

If the violation had been only somebody beating us up on the playground, that probably wouldn't change our entire life. But sexual, physical, and verbal assaults permeate every part of us.

The question makes me think of a situation I encounter professionally. I'm a ghostwriter-collaborator and have made my living at this craft for thirty-five years. Perhaps twenty times a year someone wants help in learning to write a book and comes to me for tips or sometimes has an extensive list of questions.

I hardly know how to answer except to point out that the art or craft of writing takes time—years—of hard work and serious commitment. One reason most would-be writers fail is because they stop. Give up. They often complain, "Nobody will take first-time writers. No one cares." The excuses pile up, and I heard all of them when I first started. But I persevered and it paid off.

Perseverance. Persistence. It's not a one-month rehab course. The same is true for us. The wound is deep, the healing is slow, but the result is worth it.

Faithful God, help me keep working for healing.
Don't let me make excuses and give up.

SEEKING ONE TRUSTING RELATIONSHIP

"I want one person—just one—I can trust and rely on." I wonder how many times I've heard men say those words.

It's not a bad desire; it's just not enough. We need others, and no relationship provides everything.

Some men refer to their wives as their best friend. That bothers me because it usually means that their spouses must carry all their emotional baggage and must become everything the man requires.

No one—not a single person—fulfills every shortfall. It's a terrible burden to lay on someone and expect her to be that perfect individual—the flawless, infallible one.

A healthier way is to build several relationships. Look for those worthy-of-trust individuals. *Be to them what you want them to offer you.*

For example, I have one friend who is a marvelous listener. He rarely offers advice, but it's obvious to me that he's there for me.

Another friend lovingly tells me the things I don't want to know about myself. That is, when I become vulnerable to him, he often intuits meaning behind my words and actions. When he points these things out, I'm able to see different parts of myself—what I call my shadow or backside. I'm grateful for him.

A third friend is easy to talk to and it's just as easy for me to listen to what he says.

All three are important—and there are a few others—because each provides something I need. Not one of them provides everything.

God, forgive me for feeling I need only one person in my
healing journey. Provide me with caring individuals.

FACING GUILT

"I feel so guilty," George said.

When I asked him for specifics, he could only mumble, "I don't know . . . it's just this nagging feeling." Finally, he added, "If only I had . . ." and he mentioned several things he wished he'd done.

That kind of thinking is more common than most of us realize. I stared at him and said, "You were a kid; you didn't understand; you weren't mature enough to reason the way you do today. You've had more than thirty years to live with that pain. Don't punish that little boy for being vulnerable."

Apparently shocked by my response, he blinked away tears. "I—I never thought of it that way. I've been tough on myself because I didn't tell or fight him off—"

"And he's still abusing you today, isn't he? As long as you focus on what *you* didn't do, he'll keep hurting you."

He nodded.

"Each time you feel guilty, say these words aloud to yourself: 'I am not guilty. I was an innocent child.'"

> Caring God, take away any sense of guilt. Remind
> me that, as a child, I did the best I could.

— *40* —

THE NEED TO GRIEVE

We survivors need to grieve—grieve for our lost childhood, for our painful memories, for our exploitation. Years ago, I read a proverb that went something like this:

"Those who hide their grief have no remedy for it."

In our healing journey, most of us go through a plethora of emotions, including anger and shame. And we can't neglect grief—the anguish and heartache of our stolen childhoods. We need to mourn over the energy we expended trying to free ourselves from something that wasn't our fault.

It's all right to feel sad, miserable, or distressed. We were victimized because we were young and defenseless. We wanted someone to care for us, to love us, and to accept us. What we received was none of those. And we suffered.

Grieve for that little boy. This may seem strange to you, but I've learned to talk to that little boy and say, "I'm here for you. I've suffered with you. We don't want to focus on what we might have been or what we've lost. Together we'll concentrate on what we're going to be."

Our revenge is to turn into happy, peaceful, and loving men.

God, help me honor my grief. Teach me to
mourn over my stolen childhood.

YOU'RE NOTHING

I don't recall that anyone ever said to me "You're nothing," although I believed I was worthless and a really bad kid.

My baby brother, Chuck, who I am sure was also sexually assaulted, once said—in a moment of rare insight while drunk—"I'm nobody. Nothing. Worthless. And I hate my life." We were in a park for a family gathering, and he had already downed at least three beers. Chuck abruptly turned and walked away from me.

That incident happened about two years before memories of my own abuse sneaked out of their hidden caverns. Even now I vividly remember his words and the pained expression on his face.

Since then I've met many men who accepted a message of worthlessness— some being told, others absorbing the concept. Regardless, we believed a terrible lie.

Growing up, I didn't feel loved by my parents. Nothing I did to gain their love seemed to make any difference. When I was as young as ten years old, the kids in my tough neighborhood sought me out. They trusted me, and I never understood why.

By the time I was in my teens, I had become the best friend of many schoolmates as my unconscious way to receive love. (I wasn't aware of that until I was well into the healing process.)

I particularly remember Jesse Marlin, who once asked me to keep money for him that he had saved. "If I take it home, they'll take it away from me." He also said, "I know you won't tell anyone." I didn't understand why my childhood friends like Jesse, Frankie Gile, Ronnie Larson, and Chuck Baldwin—all vague memories today—told me things they didn't tell others. Their confidence in me made me feel good—at least temporarily.

Years later I taught in public and private schools, spent six years in missionary service in Kenya, and was a pastor for fourteen years. One day I said to myself, "People like me because I'm nice to them and do things for them. Would they still like me if I didn't do that?"

In retrospect, it was my unconscious way to *earn* affection. And to earn it isn't satisfying.

When I was twenty-two years old I married Shirley Brackett, and although she knew about my family background, she didn't know about my molestation. I loved her, as much as I knew how to love, but for a long time I found it difficult to believe she truly loved me.

Once I said to her, "Even if I beat you, you'll still love me."

Shock appeared in her eyes. "You'd never beat me."

"But if I did—"

She shook her head. "I can't even imagine you doing anything to hurt me."

That was when I grasped I was loved. Because I finally realized that deep within I was unconditionally loved by one person, it strengthened me to start facing my past.

If there is any secret to feeling we're worthwhile, it's this: *we need to know we're loved.* When someone cares enough to sit beside us—to be present with us—in our pain, we know we're loved.

So how do we learn to accept the marvelous truths about ourselves? It's not easy, but it's possible. I think of 1 John 4:19, which says, "We love because [God] first loved us."

To feel loved by others, we need to trust them enough to open up about ourselves—to be transparent. For most of us, it's a risk. But it's also worth the risk.

None of us is worthless, but I can't convince anyone of that just by words. Being loved and valued by someone we care about is the only way we escape that untruth of being worthless.

Gracious God, as you help me grasp your love
for me, teach me that I'm of value.

WHO AM I?

"I didn't know who I was," Mac said to me after I spoke to a Celebrate Recovery group. "Being molested messed with my brain."

Mac didn't have a lot of formal education but he said it well. Abuse affects all parts of our lives. I'm constantly amazed in my own life when I have a jarring realization of something I say or do that connects to my abuse.

Here's an example. I recently spoke with Matt about his abuse. He made me uncomfortable because he invaded my space—standing about six inches away from me—far too close.

After a couple of minutes of discomfort, I put my hands on his shoulders as I took a step back, and said, "I'm uneasy when you stand so close." Before he could say anything, I added, "I think it speaks about your need for intimacy."

Those words rushed out of my mouth without my consciously thinking of them.

Matt turned his face away from me and stared into space for several seconds. He nodded slowly. "I know, but I can't help myself. I feel I have to move close to people, and yet they move away from me."

I thought of buzzwords like lack of boundaries to help him, but instead, I heard myself say, "I'll bet you wished someone would hug you—often."

"And when they do, I don't want to let go," he said. "And that makes them not want to hug me again."

In that moment, I realized how many times I've wanted to be held, embraced, or even touched. It became clear to me that I had felt similar needs, but I reacted differently. When I hugged, I did it with great intensity (perhaps I still do). But the difference is that back then, I tried to signal that I wanted the same intense embrace I gave them. Instead, I think I made *them* feel uncomfortable.

Like Mac, I continue to realize how much my being molested messed with my brain.

> Embracing God, I need affection. Thank you for loving
> me, and bringing people into my life who love me.

— *43* —

RAPE? ASSAULT?

A friend wrote me because he was having trouble using the word *rape*. For him, the word carried a tone of violence. "He was gentle and kind to me," my friend wrote. "So how could that be rape?"

I had gone through a similar struggle. My rapist, Mr. Lee, spoke softly, gave me small gifts, hugged me, and made me feel special. How could that be rape or assault?

And yet it was.

"It's still rape," I replied. "Call it seductive rape. Call it taking advantage of an innocent child. You were not mature enough to defend yourself or to object to the actions of an older, powerful adult."

I understood his problem with the word, because I had my own struggle with what to call my childhood experiences. My most common word is now *assault*. I refer to *abuse* and *molestation*, but those two words have been around so long that, for me, they'd lost their forcefulness and they don't show the powerful motivation of the perpetrator (even if they were gentle). I chose *assault* because it's closer to the reality of what happened to me.

Both my friend and I were children, and we were raped or assaulted by someone bigger and older. We were too naive to realize the meaning of what happened to us. We were lonely, love-starved kids who yearned for attention. Even though assaulted, we believed we were being cared about and the affection was genuine. And it felt good. Temporarily.

Now that we're older, some of us have trouble using the right word to describe the secretive attack (and we need to remind ourselves our perpetrators' actions were deliberate, planned attacks).

We're troubled by facing words like *rape* because our understanding of that term carries many violent implications. TV has filled our minds with brutal and vicious actions.

One day I realized that when I used such strong words, I was able to face the seriousness of what had been done to me. *Assault* has also pushed me a little further down the healing path, because I no longer excuse my perpetrators. It doesn't matter that they may have been victims themselves or that they might have said they couldn't help themselves.

Regardless of their pleas, they did a forceful, terrible thing to us. They raped us.

> Loving God, help me use the words that enable me
> to face the horror of my childhood victimization.

FEAR
Gary Roe

One of the most prevalent internal demons that I struggle with is fear. My fear equals a lack of safety. Most of the time, I simply do not feel safe.

There are many nights when I wake up shaking, sweating, and terrified. I have to breathe deeply and pray, asking God to reassure me that it is not happening again.

I am tired of living in fear. I am tired of worrying about everything. If I really track all the things I worry about, I begin to get a sobering picture about where my mind can run off to. Sometimes I just talk to myself out loud, expressing what I am worried about or fearful of. Thankfully, I often smile afterward, because it sounds so ridiculous. And sometimes there comes the nagging thought, *Yeah, but it happened before, lots of times. And it could happen again.* It's ugly, and I'm tired of it.

The feelings are real, and I cannot stop them from coming. I must acknowledge them—they are already there—but I do not have to let them rule. I have a choice: I can cry out to God and trust him (and ask for the ability to trust him) or I can choose to continue down the endless road of fear.

I'm learning that when I live in fear, I am not fully present to the ones I love. I am living inside my head. Things have become about me and about my survival. And it does feel like survival. I want to break out of that and really love those around me at any given moment.

I'm reminded that on the night before his crucifixion, Jesus told his disciples, "Peace I leave with you; my peace I give you. I do not give to you as the world gives. Do not let your hearts be troubled and do not be afraid" (John 14:27). The goal is not to not be afraid. The goal is that when I find myself in fear, I'll turn to him and trust him that, over time, I will experience his peace, his safety.

God, when fear grabs me, teach me to look
toward you and experience your peace.

ISOLATION IS EMOTIONAL SOLITARY CONFINEMENT

Roger Mann

Isolation is where I've lived most of my life. That's why I felt alone and sad much of the time. Even when I was in a crowd or with a group of friends I felt out of step with everyone, just not quite connecting on the level everyone else seemed to.

Abuse immediately isolated me. At first, the need for secrecy and knowing I was sharing in something no one else could know about gave me a sense of superiority. I felt special, privileged (for a while anyway). Later I felt used and eventually worthless.

At first we can feel pretty special, but later we realize we've taken on a burden we can't seem to throw off. I ended up feeling different and weird, and thinking no one else could possibly have those kinds of thoughts, feelings, or desires. After that came the longing to be normal—whatever that was supposed to mean. I was left outside, stealing glances at other families who seemed happy and normal.

That led to a lot of overcompensating and arrogance and not a little amount of anger, which I tried to repress unsuccessfully. I felt trapped, alone, and unable to break free to interact with my closest friends. There was always a wall there that I couldn't tear down.

With God's help and help from those who love me and understand, I'm learning new ways to break through the barriers. I appreciate their patience because the trust thing is difficult for me to navigate after all these years.

Ever-caring God, remind me that it's not
too late for you to heal me.

WHY DIDN'T GOD STOP THE ABUSE?

Sometimes the question comes out as, "Where was God?"

When we ask such questions, we imply that if God is good, nothing bad should happen to us—or at least nothing bad should happen to the innocent. Life just doesn't work that way. I've been reading the Bible for more than fifty years and the promises of God are to be with us in our pain and not to shield us. For example, "Even when I walk through the darkest valley, I will not be afraid, for you are close beside me" (Ps. 23:4 NLT).

Here are two oft-quoted verses: "Do not fear, for I have redeemed you; I have summoned you by name; you are mine. When you pass through the waters, I will be with you; and when you pass through the rivers, they will not sweep over you. When you walk through the fire, you will not be burned; the flames will not set you ablaze" (Isa. 43:1–2).

I wish God had protected me during childhood. I hate the pain I've had to go through. But now—after dealing with my issues for years—I can look back and thank God for taking me through those terrible times. He didn't let me give up, and I'm healthier today. However, that's not all: I can help others in their pain because I can feel what they feel.

Too often we forget the purpose of our ordeals. Here's how the apostle Paul looks at it: "Praise be to the God and Father of our Lord Jesus Christ, the Father of compassion and the God of all comfort, who comforts us in all our troubles, so that we can comfort those in any trouble with the comfort we ourselves receive from God" (2 Cor. 1:3–4).

By suffering, we come out stronger and more sensitive to the needs of others. We can wrap our arms around the hurting because we know how it feels to be hurt.

I don't know why God didn't intervene; I do know
that I can intervene when others are in pain.
Lord, help me to intervene to help others.

ANGER AGAINST OURSELVES

Counselor Dr. Gordon Grose refers to a study of 17,000 people in which experts analyzed the effect of Adverse Childhood Experiences (ACE). They examined ten categories, including physical and sexual abuse, and they followed the lives of those affected.

"Fifty years after those traumatic events, the study matched the person's current state of health and well-being against their ACE score. . . . Results revealed the strong relationship between increasing ACE scores and chronic depression in men and women in later life."[7]

Grose also stresses the correlation between increased ACE scores, increased health costs, and decreased life expectancy. "People tend to respond to early injustice with lifelong self-destructive tendencies. It's as if they tell themselves, *If I can't make someone else pay, my body will.*"[8]

The lesson for us is that the pain and anger of childhood will come out in some form—unconsciously. The more obvious way is anger at others. If we assume the results are correct, what do we do?

The answers vary for each of us, but this much is clear: we need help for those outcroppings. Too often we treat anger as something different and separate from our abuse. But it's really a symptom.

Too often we're angry at ourselves. We become the receptacle for the anger and we don't need that.

God, free me from being angry at myself. Remind
me that you love me and you have set me free.

WHY DID I GO BACK?

Roger Mann

I have shared with only two people that I did go back home—long after I no longer needed to, and long after he was probably through with me. After the divorce from my first wife, I spent a holiday weekend with my parents. That first evening, Dad told me I could have his bedroom and he would sleep in their camper/trailer.

Later, I turned out the light to go to sleep. Tired as I was, I found myself alert and lying once again in the dark, a ten-year-old kid in a thirty-three-year-old body. Sometime after midnight, I heard familiar sounds outside my door. Without thinking, I pulled back the covers so he could see me.

Why would I do that? At that point in my life, I was well aware of what we were doing and how wrong it was. What did I want/need from him? It was just as unsatisfying as it was twenty-three years earlier, but now it was embarrassing, humiliating, and I ended up feeling like crap. Why did I feel the need to surrender access to me? Was it familiarity, guilt, a chance to rewrite history? Or maybe I thought it was a chance to talk about what we were doing.

Of course, the next day it was as if nothing had happened. He was my father and the pastor of my church all my life.

How long would this go on?

Dad took that terrible dilemma out of my hands with his suicide years afterward. But I'm still left with the question of why I went back, and whether I would have continued.

Not many of us incest survivors have to face those questions and doubts, but I understand the terrible pull to accept that phone call, answer that text, or open the door to someone who I know is going to hurt me.

> God, don't let me go back again in action or
> memory. Keep me going forward. Every day.

DON'T LET THEM SAY IT

Most of us encounter individuals who pry into our lives or ask questions that trigger memories, or they're just unaware of how offensive their remarks sound. Some do it ignorantly because they don't know what else to say.

The next time someone says something inappropriate, we need to be able to quietly but firmly reply with something simple such as, "I don't want to talk about that."

One of my friends smiles and says to the inquisitive, "Can you keep a secret?" He told me that the other person always answers yes, so he replies, "So can I," and says no more. They usually laugh. If they don't get it, he walks away.

That approach may not work for everyone (and it's not something I'm comfortable doing), but I suggest we find simple but kind responses to irresponsible statements. I remind myself that because they're rude or insensitive I don't have to mimic their behavior.

The worst question I've been asked was at an informal gathering and a man I scarcely knew came up to me. He said he heard that I had been molested and I affirmed that I had been.

"Did you like it?"

I was so offended, I stared at the man. "Excuse me, please," I said and walked across the room.

"I guess you didn't," he said as I walked away.

I'm not saying I handled it well, but I refused to give in to his voyeuristic question.

Each of us has a right to privacy and to protect ourselves. In fact, it's more than that. I consider it a sacred responsibility to protect ourselves from such insensitive people.

> Wise God, remind me that they may ask,
> but I'm not required to answer.

BY NOW . . .

"By now," a pastor friend said to me, "you should be over all that. It happened so long ago."

"Do you have some kind of way to set time limits?"

"No, that's not what I meant," he said. "Just that, well, it happened when you were a kid."

"Time isn't the healer," I said angrily, defensively, and ready to walk away from him. He kept trying to say that he didn't *really* mean those words.

"You're digging a deeper hole each time you open your mouth to explain," I said. "Right now I'm angry." I regret saying the next words, but I did. "It must be nice to be someone like you without hang-ups or problems that began in childhood and still continue to trouble you throughout your life."

The shock on his face told me I had touched something in him.

"I apologize," he said and told me his story of growing up with two bright, ambitious parents who seemed to treat him more as a trophy than their child.

I don't know if he ever understood my pain or if I fully understood his. But his last words to me were, "I know only two kinds of people who had perfect childhoods: habitual liars and people who can't remember."

> Lord God, I'm not a habitual liar, and I remember the pain.
> I also know I'm healing at my own pace. Thank
> you for helping me on that journey.

GAINING STRENGTH

"Every time I overcome something from my painful past, I become stronger and more prepared for the next self-discovery." I put those words in quotes, because I can't remember who wrote that to me or exactly the way he said it, but that was the gist.

That's also a general life principle, isn't it? Each victory, no matter how small, prepares us for the next. For example, in 2007, our house burned down and we lost everything. While waiting for the fire trucks to arrive, I watched everything we owned being destroyed.

One of the first things that popped into my mind was these words, "I've been preparing for this." It wasn't something I'd thought of until that moment, but it was true. I did a quick review of my life and various trials. I also realized that if the fire had happened twenty years earlier, I wouldn't have been able to handle it nearly so well. Instead, I'd probably ask questions such as, "How did I fail you, Lord?" or "God, are you punishing me?"

The other thing that came to me that day was a quotation from the book of Job in the Old Testament. Everything, including his children, had been killed or destroyed. His wife urged him to curse God and die. Instead, Job said, "Will we receive good from God but not also receive bad?" (Job 2:10 CEB).

Each time I go through a painful experience in my healing, I try to remind myself that I've been preparing for the present agony. I also remind myself that such insights and experiences don't come until we can handle them.

Some might want to argue with that last statement, but I stand by it. Some give up or go into depression, but I believe we have those experiences only when we *can* handle them.

Strong and holy God, enable me to accept the hardships each day. Use those difficult times to prepare me for future troubles.

WHY AM I NOT HEALED BY NOW?

After we've been treading along the painful winding path toward whole-ness, many of us look ahead and see how far we have yet to go. It's like hiking up a mountain, and just as we reach the summit, we stare ahead and realize that to reach the destination means we keep walking toward another mountain peak.

"There's always another mountain to climb," I groaned after about a year. Then I remembered the testimonies I used to hear from members of AA. After they told their stories of debauchery and agony, they went on to express the peace and joy they had experienced since their sobriety. Their presentations made it sound as if they had been totally healed.

They weren't healed. Some of them held up their tokens to proclaim their sobriety. And many of them didn't go back to alcohol. None of them had everything figured out. The best members of AA would say to me that the journey was still one day at a time. The most victorious were able to say they were closer to a healthier life. None of them ever talked about arrival.

As I wrote this, I thought about the death of my wife. During the first months the loss was intense—but I expected that. I grieved, as I knew I would. What I didn't expect was that the grief process went on a long, long time. That helped me realize that only those things that mean a great deal to us keep us crying out.

We tend to think, *My happiness, my joy, and deep contentment will be the result of taking this torturous journey, so I'm willing to stay on the bumpy, on-going trail.* If you're agonizing over the journey yet ahead, perhaps you need to pause and look backward to see how far you've come.

> Lord, remind me to ponder how far I've already come.
> I can say, "I haven't arrived, but I'm well on the way."
> And even now, you've made it worth the effort.

DISTORTED RELATIONSHIPS

About a decade ago my friend Gerald died of cancer. What I remember most about our relationship was his attitude toward women. I didn't know all his history, except that he detested his mother. I don't know if there had been sexual assault (he never said, and I never pried). I do know she abused him verbally and possibly physically.

The significance of that—and I think it's often true no matter the form of abuse by a female—is the distorted perception of women in general. Not once did Gerald ever talk about women in a caring tone. He mentioned women he had dated, and he'd say things such as, "I know she's slept with a dozen men."

His references weren't limited to them, but he seemed to tag every woman as immoral. We were still good friends when he married either his third or fourth wife, and she was one of the finest women I'd ever known. He made accusations about her I was sure were wrong, but he insisted he *knew* the bad things she had done.

That's what I mean by distorted relationships. One time I said, "You've never had a satisfactory relationship with a woman, have you?"

"Not yet," he answered.

The last I saw Gerald before he moved to another state, he was still married to the woman he had vilified. And I thought, "It will never last."

It didn't.

I tell this about Gerald because he lived and died without facing his distorted view of women. That's one of the sad results of abuse.

Lord, help me face my pain because I want to be free from it.

THE CONSEQUENCES

We survivors have been damaged—which is why we struggle. Perhaps the most serious injury involves our battle in trusting others. We read mostly about those who can't trust anyone. But some of us remain susceptible, almost as if we're saying, "Take advantage of me." As I look back, the physical and verbal abuse might have been even more profound than the sexual.

One of my survivor-friends said, "I tend to believe everyone until they fail or let me down in some way." He went on to say that when a person fails one time, then he's unable to trust them again. Once hurt, he can't forget what they've done.

Most of the time, naiveté described me. Even today as an adult, people occasionally castigate me for trusting others and call me too trusting. For a long time, my response was, "I can't help it."

And for many years I couldn't. I've had to work quite hard at questioning the motivations and intentions of others. The other extreme (and more common response) is assuming everyone wants to exploit or hurt us.

Those are all outcomes of our stolen and broken childhoods.

◆　◆　◆

I'll pass on something that helped me. When I have any strong sense of faith in or doubt about anyone, I try to wait until I can get alone and process it. *What was going on inside me,* I ask myself, *that I had that reaction? Was it my self-protective inner wisdom? Was it the old pattern of willing to be exploited?*

Not that an answer pops up immediately, because it rarely does. Instead, the tendency is for me to quote a famous line from the 1943 film, *Casablanca,* "Round up the usual suspects."

When I realize that I'm doing that, and can't find a clear answer for myself, I get with one of my friends to help me discern what I feel.

Lord, my abuse has powerful ramifications. Help
me defeat my warped understanding.

— 55 —

RUNNING FROM THE PAST

When my wife died, my friend Gary Roe sent me a copy of his book *Heartbroken: Healing from the Loss of a Spouse*. Much of what he writes applies to healing from abuse as well as from the loss of a spouse.

One sentence stayed with me long after reading: "As we allow ourselves to feel the pain, our hearts will begin to heal."[9]

Wonderful words, but the problem comes for many with the statement, *allow* ourselves to feel the pain. That's what many won't or can't do.

"It hurts too much," is a common response.

Of course it's painful and traumatic. If it didn't hurt, the healing would have taken place long ago.

Instead of facing the situations, too many medicate themselves so they can run from their past—and it's often not a conscious choice but an attempt to cope. Some resort to drugs, others cut off their emotions. My medication was busyness. For years, I was a driven man but was not aware of it. "That's just the way I am," I often defended myself (and believed my words).

Gradually, I learned to stop running away (which is what my busyness was accomplishing). I wrote *gradually* because as with most of us survivors, I moved slowly into awareness.

After I became aware of my choice of medication, I decided to do something about my drivenness. I read everything I could on how to live in the present and slow down. Taking time to read, in itself, was part of my process. Yet slowing down was painful because the effort forced me to think. *And to feel.*

I stayed with it and I'm making progress. The struggle to run from my pain was useless. I couldn't outrun my childhood trauma. But I could face it.

And I do.

God, help me not to run from my pain. Help me face and
grow from my past and be thankful for your healing power.

THEIR INNER CIRCLES

Over the years, other men have said to me, "You're my best friend," and they sincerely meant it. None of them was *my* best friend. That's not to blame them, but to admit I didn't know how to open up and trust another man.

Several men included me in their inner circle; I wish I could have included them in mine. I wanted to be open and transparent to them, but I couldn't. My trust had been stolen as a child, and for me to expose my inner feelings was to suffer the abuse again. It seemed safer to lock up my past.

I had my inner circle—which consisted only of myself. For a long time, I couldn't even be transparent to my wife, and yet she was the most loving and trusting soul I knew.

My first breakthrough came through a friend named Martin (and I've since told him). At age fifteen, his drunken mother seduced him. After he told me, I marveled that he trusted me with that deep, deep secret.

Another man, the late Steve Grubmann, assaulted by a foster parent, cried as he talked of his trauma forty years after the fact, but I sensed he experienced some healing just from the act of sharing.

Martin and Steve included me in their inner circles, even if they didn't use those words. They also opened the door for me by modeling trusting behavior.

When I haltingly told my wife about my childhood assault, I expected rejection and revulsion. Instead, Shirley said, "I'm sorry," and hugged me. That same day, I told David, who later became my best friend. By the way he listened, I knew he accepted my pain. He didn't try to fix me; he simply accepted me.

Shirley and David were the first members of my inner circle and because of them, I learned to invite others into it. As I openly spoke of my pain, I was giving others permission to face their past and join my inner circle.

Loving God, teach me to form a loving circle
by trusting others to care for me.

NO SELF-JUDGING ALLOWED

On a hand-painted sign I saw those words, "No self-judging allowed," in a friend's den. "I think I understand the words," I said, "but why the sign?"

"Yes!" Alan said. "I made that for what I hoped would be an opportunity to tell people about my abuse." For almost two years he had kept the words posted, and only a handful of visitors had asked about it.

"It began in a group therapy session," he said. Alan was condemning himself for allowing an older boy to sodomize him. Before he sought help, he talked about allowing the horrible things done to him.

Another member of the group interrupted him. "Don't you have any compassion for that little boy? He did what he had to do to survive."

When Alan started to protest, others in the group also urged him to be kind to the abused child.

"I had been in and out of therapy for addictions," he said, "but I realized I hadn't been kind to my young inner self."

"You survived because of him," one man said. "You may have done things you're ashamed of now, but that hurt, despised kid kept you alive."

For quite a while we talked before Alan said, "I put up that sign to remind me and to help me to be kind and understanding to the memory of the child I used to be."

As I stared at the three words, he added, "Every night, even now, I stare at my reflection in the mirror and think of the eight-year-old boy and say to him, 'Thank you for helping me survive.'"

"I like that idea," I said.

"I no longer have to say, 'No self-judging allowed.' Now I leave the sign up in the den, hoping it will help others."

> God, thank you for the courageous child I used to be.
> Thank you for the overcoming adult I've become.

NEEDING SUPPORT

We battle alone but we also need to know there are others who support us and pray for us. We can ask the questions, and others can make suggestions, but it's still a personalized, individual battle that only we can fight for ourselves.

Others can help by their presence and caring. One of the places I often go when I need support is the Bible. When I was going through a dark period, I read Exodus 17. In this story, the Israelites are fighting their first battle after leaving Egypt. The Amalekites attack and Joshua leads the people into battle.

Moses stands on a mountain with his hands raised as a symbol of victory. Joshua's troops are winning. Before long, Moses' arms grow tired and he starts to lower them. When he drops his arms, the Amalekites prevail. Two men, Aaron and Hur, make Moses sit on a boulder and they get on either side of him and hold up his arms. The three of them stay in that position until Joshua thoroughly defeats their enemy.

Holding up our tired arms draws a powerful image for me. We get frustrated, confused, and feel lost. One of my problems was that as memories came back, my deep resistance was to say, "That's only your imagination. That's not true." But when I told the two people who held my arms, they helped me accept the truthfulness of my flashbacks and memories.

When I doubted that I'd ever get healthy, they assured me that I would. They kept those weak, weary, and discouraged arms held up until I won my biggest battles. All of us need those caring people who are there to lift up our arms.

Who is holding up your arms?

Powerful God, help me trust others to hold my
arms, especially when the battles rage.

WEARING MASKS

Some experts talk about the masks we wear around others. Most of us don't consciously put on disguises, but we submerge our true feelings underneath a smile because it makes life safer. We can hide under a grin and say to the world, "I'm happy. I'm happy."

Or we can conceal ourselves with a glare that silently says, "Don't get too close." The man who always has a new joke and never gets serious may be afraid that you'll make him vulnerable and he's not ready to be transparent.

In some form, all of us wear masks and we don't expose our inner pain or emotions to everyone. But for those of us who were abused, if our masks slip, we unintentionally reveal a glimpse of who we are. Another way to say it is that the façade often shows *who we'd like to be.*

Before I dealt with my abuse, others referred to me as a happy person. That was true—*sometimes*. I wanted to be happy and to enjoy my life. During the six years I served as a missionary in Kenya, one of the names they called me was *Omore*, which means a happy person.

That was part of who I was—the positive side I was willing to show openly.

Our concealment can also be unintentional deception and we may not be aware that we're hiding part of ourselves. Those masks aren't about relating to or impressing others. Think of them as weapons of *protection*. We weren't always aware of not being our true selves; it was our way to retreat from our pain.

"I feel like I'm so many different people," Albert said at the second meeting of a state-sponsored group of men who had survived sexual assault in childhood. He explained that he behaved a certain way with close friends, differently with casual acquaintances. "At work, I don't act like I do when I'm with friends."

"Maybe you need a handful of masks to survive," one man said.

We discussed Albert's situation and we finally admitted that all of us wear masks. Like Albert, we relate to people in a social setting differently than we do to people who don't know us well.

"Who is the real me?" Albert asked. "That's what troubles me and brought me to this group. I don't know which one is real."

"Probably all of them," I said. Not everyone agreed with me, but I believe we show only parts of ourselves at any one time. Another way to say it is that we conceal parts of ourselves when we *need* to do so. That is, we may be friendly, even outgoing, but we get to choose how much we want to self-reveal.

The less we trust others, the more we feel the need to conceal to convince people we're who we purport to be. It's safe, and it's not difficult to deceive.

It may be easy, but that's not freedom. Perhaps it borders on hypocrisy, but we once-abused kids may need to size up the situation before the safe side of us shows itself. For me, it's not whether to wear masks—because we all do at certain times—but my need is *to be aware that I'm suppressing myself behind a mask*.

One of the most poignant comments I've ever received came from a man I didn't know well. His daughter came to a mentoring clinic for writers that I conducted in 2010. She decided to come because her father told her, "That man is real."

That's my goal: to be real all the time. It's not easy, but I know a man who was always real and he's my model.

His name is Jesus.

Lord, help me to be transparent and honest with everyone.

HIS ANGER

At a writers conference I met Jeff. We spoke over lunch and I liked him. He told me about the book he was writing and asked me if I'd look at a few pages. I said yes.

That evening I read the first nine pages, and the prose wasn't very good. It showed promise but lacked the polished skill of professional writing. Something else bothered me but I couldn't figure out what it was.

The next day at breakfast, I prepared a nice, innocuous statement about the book needing work. To my surprise, the first words out of my mouth were, "Why are you so enraged? You seem to be angry at everybody and everything."

He stared at me for a long time, saying nothing, but the tightness of his jaw told me I was correct. He dropped his head and said, "I'm angry a lot."

"It shows in your writing," I said, realizing that was what I hadn't been able to identify the night before.

I've met other men like Jeff. They tend to focus their anger in three different ways. The most obvious one is toward the person who abused them. Or they're angry at themselves—because they "let it happen." A third target is the adults who didn't protect him from the predator.

Sometimes it's all three. I've met a few once-molested men who are generally angry at the world. Sometimes they live a long time in denial of the abuse or they sublimate it. It's as if the anger goes underground and comes to the surface in an area where it's safe to be mad.

Many of us male survivors know about anger. We haven't always known the reason for our anger, but we knew the feeling. As we face our anger and determine to do something about it, healing takes place.

> God, I'm angry—often. Help me face my anger.
> Free me from that dark, powerful emotion.

STEALING SECOND BASE

I don't remember the first time I heard or read this truism: you can't steal second base and keep your foot on first.

The impact of those words is that the healing journey is risky. Any healthy survivor will echo those words. Once we open the door to our painful childhood, we never know what's going to come out.

For example, I hadn't cried since I was eleven years old; I started my healing journey forty years later. Then I cried—almost every day for weeks. I'd see something about mistreatment on TV or read a scene in a book, and the tears would flow.

More than the tears, I began seeing characteristics about myself I didn't like—qualities others could see but had previously been hidden from me. It hurt for me to face them and say to myself, "Yes, that's true."

Hard. Risky. The safer, easier path is denial. But I had lived in that community too long not to know the problems there.

The acute responses to my self-knowledge (i.e., the intense pain) lasted months. But I prevailed. I can only thank God, my wife, and my best friend because they were there when I needed them. Even so, it was *my* pain, *my* traumatic past. And as one wise survivor said to me, "The only way out is through. You'll never be free of the pain until you reexperience it."

When I took my foot off first base, I risked being hurt, humiliated, and misunderstood and I just kept going.

So can you. Move your foot off first base. Take the risk.

God, help me take risks—that's called faith, and it honors you.

NON-SUICIDAL SELF-INJURY
Tom Scales

Many survivors of childhood sexual abuse are brainwashed to believe they can't make good decisions for themselves. I was one of those children. During the period of abuse, the predator subtly and deceitfully convinces the victims they're responsible and complicit in the behavior. Even though the victims are children, they're programmed to believe that the acts were consensual. As a result, the victims assume a responsibility and guilt that become serious problems in the healing process.

Thus, if they feel complicit in the evil, their sense of self is severely damaged. On some level, they see themselves saturated in deceit and lies. Over time, they build up rage and self-hatred that turn into self-destructive behavior.

I had never heard the term *non-suicidal self-injury* until I started to understand my past and my behavior.

One of the most difficult steps in healing for me was to separate my behavior and my responsibilities from those of the predator. I had to remind myself that I had been a child with the emotional and mental capabilities of a child.

I finally understood that I had no power, no control, and no method of escape. To heal, I had to become truly free of the control and influence of the predators. I had to accurately understand that I was in no way complicit in the evil that was done to me.

I was allowing men who had been dead for years to continue to control my life. That's when I realized I needed to forgive all my predators, and do so without reservation. As long as I carried the anger, rage, and desire for vengeance toward them, those feelings ate at my soul and discolored my self-perceptions.

It took me time to understand that forgiveness didn't free them from accountability, but released *me*.

My forgiveness didn't liberate them from the prospects of an excruciating final judgment and consequences; it removed from my hands the role of judge, jury, and executioner.

Forgiveness doesn't relieve the perpetrators from their accountability, and it's not a license for more abuse. Forgiving must come from our hearts. Only then was I free to be *me*, and that *me* is now someone I respect and love.

God, help me to forgive—totally and completely—and to remind myself that you are the final judge of all our hearts.

LOSING MY FAITH

"I lost my faith, if I really had any, when I was nine," Nick's email began. He said the youth pastor of his church befriended him. "That was cool because my dad and mom were always working or lying in front of the TV. My pastor took me to ball games and taught me wrestling techniques."

The rest of the story is familiar to many of us. One evening after everyone else had left the church gym, Nick and the youth pastor went to the showers. He hugged Nick, held him, and began to fondle him.

"I was scared and didn't know what to do. He was supposed to be like my best friend." Nick didn't resist. "But I hated myself and I hated God for letting that sicko do that to me."

He never went to church again.

Hundreds of men can tell similar stories. Rape of a child is a horrible thing but it seems even worse when it's someone who represents God or the church.

"God let it happen to me," they say. "If God loved me, why did he let it happen?"

I don't have an answer about why any catastrophe or pain occurs. Why do people die in accidents? Develop incurable diseases?

It's too simplistic to blame God or an unobservant parent, but it's a good way to avoid facing what happened and learning to be free and victorious. Instead, I hope you'll say, "Yes, it happened, and I've survived. Now I want to do more than survive—I want to overcome the pain." And as we gain healing, it can also rekindle our faith in a loving God.

I wasn't involved in the church during my childhood, but I do know this. Once I faced my painful assault, I cried out to God to help me because I couldn't do it on my own. One of my survivor-friends quotes Philippians 4:13 every day, "For I can do everything through Christ, who gives me strength" (NLT).

Some turn to God because there's nowhere else to turn. My friend Nick, who lost his faith, wrote that he hadn't fully returned to God, but he has started to attend a charismatic church in Ohio.

His final words were, "I'm creeping back into the faith."

Lord, for those who feel betrayed or let down by the church, remind us that you are the always-faithful one.

SHATTER THE SILENCE

I titled my blog *Shattering the Silence* (www.menshatteringthesilence.blog spot.com), and several readers have commented on the title. Phillip wrote, "I wish I had shattered the silence earlier, instead of staying in bondage."

He attended a prestigious boarding school for boys. Phillip's dorm monitor, two years his senior, befriended him. Phillip went into detail about the things that happened before the sexual abuse began.

He wondered if he was the only one abused by the older boy. "I didn't ask because I was afraid that if I was the only one, I'd be mocked and picked on by my peers."

Just before his last year in boarding school, two years after the abuser had graduated, Phillip told his parents. They were shocked, but they believed him. "I didn't realize how much Mom and Dad loved me until then," he said.

It was too late to do anything to the abuser, but with his parents' help, he connected with other victims. None of them had ever told anyone.

Phillip shattered the silence, and it was a brave thing to do. I want to encourage more men to take such courageous action.

We can tell our stories. We need to tell our stories. When we do that as individuals or in groups, we are embracing other men who need to speak up.

Will you commit to shattering the silence?

Lord, help me to shatter the silence for
myself, and to help other survivors.

FACING MY SIN

His name is Mike and he emailed me his story (which I've condensed).

The deacon, who was also my Sunday school teacher, started visiting our home to help me understand the Bible. My folks liked him because he was friendly, and so did I.

At first. But that changed. He molested me and kept doing it every week for about two years.

You know what he told me? He said I was a terrible sinner and I was heading straight to hell but he was there to help me get rid of evil thoughts and be pure. It sounds crazy now, but I did what he told me and that was supposed to make me into a good kid.

Mike added, "Four weeks ago, I told my wife, 'He lied. He was the sinner!'"

"Of course he was." She seemed surprised I hadn't figured that out before.

I thought I was the one who had failed God and had been evil. For more than twenty years I hated myself because I believed his terrible lies.

God, thank you for helping me realize that my perpetrator
was the sinner. I was only a child—and a victim.
Now I'm an overcomer because of your grace.

GOING IT ALONE

The great American tradition is to honor and applaud those who handle life on their own—the Clint Eastwood/John Wayne heroic types. They didn't need anyone and survived without help from anyone else.

Really?

Maybe in books and films it works that way, but I don't know anyone like that who's truly happy by living totally alone and without anyone's assistance. I believe God created us for companionship (and it doesn't have to be romantic).

In recent years, a number of films have been labeled *bromedy*—where two men join together for a common goal and become friends in the process.

And yet, in our culture, the ideal persists of the silent type who needs no one.

That has never fit me. I haven't wanted to travel through life alone. I needed people and can't remember when I wasn't aware of that. I'm a highly emotional person and my late wife was my anchor. Many times, I was ready to break off from friends, change jobs, or move on in various phases of my life. Shirley was the calm one. She didn't argue or yell; she helped me realize I was making an emotional decision and not a careful, reasoned one.

More than anything else, Shirley taught me that I didn't have to take the lonesome road. Until her death, she was always there to hold my hand. Even more, she helped me grasp God's presence in my life. Psalm 16:8 reads, "I know the Lord is always with me. I will not be shaken, for he is right beside me" (NLT).

I no longer have Shirley, but the Lord remains with me and I have friends I can call or visit. I don't have to take that road marked *Alone*.

Neither do you.

It may require effort and some level of risk, but there are individuals

God places in our lives who willingly walk by our side when we have to move through troubled, dark places.

> Faithful God, remind me often that *you*
> are with me every moment.

WHY I DRANK

"When I was fifteen, I drank my first beer and then my second. It was strange but I didn't worry about anything. I had fun and it seemed like everything I said was witty." That's how Peter, a Southern Baptist pastor, started his email to me.

He went on to write that drinking kept him detached from his emotions. "When I was twenty-one, I almost washed out of college. What I thought was witty my career counselor told me was silly and often incoherent."

Peter went to an AA meeting to please his counselor so he could finish the semester and stay in college. An older man in the meeting said he had been an alcoholic for fifteen years. Then he added, "It was the only way I could forget that I had been abused."

That sentence clicked! Peter wrote, "I felt as if someone had punched me in the gut. That's when I knew why I liked getting drunk. I could forget."

Peter never took another drink, because he didn't need the booze. He graduated from college. "I wasn't at the top of the class, but I was at least part of the class."

He not only became sober, but he found a therapist who helped him cope with the trauma of childhood abuse. He's now a pastor in Iowa and has gotten his church to start a Celebrate Recovery group.

Peter is living proof that, with divine help, we can overcome our pain, help others on their journey, and move toward wholeness.

> God, I was a victim and medicated my pain in unhealthy
> ways. Give me your divine help and health. Remind
> me that your love is the only medication I need.

GRIEVING
Roger Mann

I'm reading your book *Not Quite Healed*. So much of it reads like my life. That said, the chapter on grieving really tore me up. As I read it, I realized that I'd never grieved what happened to me and the subsequent effects and their impact on my life.

It wasn't just the molestation. That in itself was bad and went on for decades. It wasn't just the lies I was told, or came to believe, or even those I told myself. It was also the person of my father.

He was a Bible-thumping, legalistic, fire-and-brimstone preacher, teacher, evangelist, and pastor—the essence of God incarnate to me. I believed every word he preached. When his words didn't add up in his actions, it caused great confusion in my immature young mind. I felt betrayed not only by him, but by God himself.

For decades, I lived full of contradictions and conflict and in dreaded fear that I would turn out like him. I was a man of two minds and very unstable. Then he had the nerve to die and leave me that way.

And not just die, he had to get himself caught with another child relative. In his fear and despair, he killed my mother in her sleep, then took his own life, leaving me a note and the mess to deal with.

In having to cope with everything, I had to keep it together and get things done because everyone else, except my wife, was a basket case. I had no time to grieve. For the next two years, I blamed myself for not saying something sooner, not warning people, not confronting him, and not saving my mother's life.

Even now I sit here writing this with no emotion. My irritability, anger, rage—all inappropriate to daily life circumstances—I see now as evidence that I have not dealt with this. For years, I didn't understand why I couldn't control my anger. Now I see that I can't go on like this. I need to process all the pain that I have suppressed.

God, whatever I've held back, make it clear to me and set me free.

MIRROR IMAGE

This morning as I came out of the shower I stared at my legs in the mirror. "You're skinny," I said to my mirror image. Perhaps that doesn't sound like much to most people. I am thin, and people have long teased me about it.

However, when I peered into a mirror in the past I never saw skinny. The image that stared back at me wasn't obese but he sure could drop twenty-five pounds. (A disclaimer: I've never been on a diet, even though that reflection told me I was too heavy.)

Years ago, I read that bulimics saw themselves as grossly overweight and I wasn't bulimic or anorexic. I was just a chubby guy. I lived with that perception most of my adult life.

When that distorted mirror image disappeared, I have no idea, but I think it was about two years ago. I stood in front of a full-length mirror wearing nothing but briefs. I stared at myself and marveled. How did I get so thin? (FYI, I'm five feet seven inches tall and weigh 135 pounds.)

What I saw for years wasn't reality—I know that now. But it shocked me to realize that I had "seen" and accepted the distorted image. I tried to explain my distortion to a close friend and he didn't seem to get it.

But for me, truly seeing my thin body was one of the most exciting and positive inner proofs of my healing. As I saw my body reflected accurately, it made me realize I was now seeing many things differently. And I like whom I see.

God, remind me of the words from "Amazing Grace"
that say, "I once was blind, but now I see." You have
opened my eyes to see myself more clearly.

FACING THE TRUTH

Something I've heard more than once in my recovery journey is that I needed to admit to myself that I had been sexually molested.

Simple. Direct. But three words stick out to me: *admit to myself*. Since that day, I've thought of those words often. Many men struggle over those three words for a long time. They may not realize all the implications (who does?) of admitting the abuse, but they probably sense they've started trying to swim in the ocean and they're not sure they'll ever find the shore again. They're scared—maybe as scared as when the abuse began.

Admit it to yourself. Say aloud, "It happened to me. I was victimized by someone older and bigger than I was."

That's where it starts. Once a man can admit to himself that it actually happened, he puts his foot on the path marked Healing Journey Lane.

> Lord, it happened to me. No matter how many times I try to
> tell myself it didn't, I know the truth. And you have promised
> that the truth will set us free. Please set me free, Lord.

WRITE A LETTER

Many mutual-help groups and therapists propose methods for molested survivors to move toward greater freedom. Recently someone suggested we write a letter to our abuser, whether the person is living or dead. They don't suggest we send it, only write it.

My advice: If it helps, do it. Try it and if you find yourself unable to complete it, be kind to yourself and say, "This doesn't work for me."

But it might.

Others have recommended speaking into a tape recorder. Writing in a journal. A friend named Greg used to hike in the mountains and when he was certain no one was around, he screamed and shouted at his perpetrator. He did that four or five times and it worked for Greg because he said, "I got it out of my system."

The method we use doesn't seem to be as important as doing something to face our hurt and anger and put it into words.

I'm a fast but not particularly accurate typist. When something bothers me, I have two major methods that work for me. One is to write it down—in a journal, an email, or maybe only a Word document that I'll later delete. I vomit out the venom and anger. The other is to ask a caring friend to listen to me without offering advice or a solution.

What works for you?

God, help me figure out the method that works
for me to move ahead in my healing journey.

DRUGS PROBABLY SAVED YOUR LIFE

Jacob, a former addict, wrote me, "I stayed zapped and blocked from my feelings for nine years. When I decided to face my issues, my therapist said, 'Your drug addiction probably saved your life.'"

The email went on to say that Jacob was convinced the only reason he hadn't killed himself was that the street drugs made the pain bearable.

"Then one day a dude I grew up with invited me to Celebrate Recovery. He had been on booze but got sober and stayed that way. And I saw the difference in his life."

Jacob said he went to his first Celebrate Recovery meeting and didn't like it very much, but he promised his friend he would go back at least once more.

Here's his comment about his second visit: "In the small group, one man spoke about being abused by a neighbor. As I listened, I felt he was talking about me. I started to cry."

Jacob went on to say he hasn't been on drugs for nearly two years. "I'm happy being sober. And alive."

Lord, I'm alive because you have a greater purpose for me.
Help me sense that purpose and faithfully follow you.

CHANGING THE PAST?
Mark Cooper

Standing in my kitchen, I feel the tiredness of this old house. Almost a decade ago I moved back into my childhood home to take care of my ailing parents. They are gone now; I'm still here.

This house is where my sexual, emotional, and religious abuse and physical neglect took place. During those years, the house wasn't ever clean or orderly. The walls were dirty with faded paint and torn, greasy wallpaper. The kitchen ceiling had a gaping hole surrounded by sagging plaster. Old linoleum floors were cracked and peeling.

There've been a lot of changes made to the house since then. I keep it (mostly) clean and neat. Dirty walls have been updated with fresh paint. The ceiling's been replaced. The floor covering is new. On the surface, there is little similarity to the house I grew up in. But no amount of remodeling will change the reality of what occurred within these 1,100 square feet.

Many abuse victims try to cover up the damage done to their souls and bodies by pursuing job promotions or more degrees; by investing blood, sweat, and tears into building a killer physique; or by changing relationships or burying themselves in addictions. I've been there. (Not the killer physique part.)

No matter how much effort we pour into making ourselves look good or successful, or how much we try to make our pain stop, we still know that underneath the many layers is a scared child wanting to be loved and accepted. Our hearts are broken.

My heart is healing as I open up my pain and memories to trusted friends and my Celebrate Recovery group. I'm changing for the better as I share what was done to me and admit the wrong choices I made trying to fix myself. I've formed friendships with other men who understand abuse. My relationship with God is growing.

Although the facts of my past won't change, my heart is healing. Repainting the walls of my house doesn't change its core structure; the healing of my heart *is* rebuilding my core. I accept that I am a man God has created with value and worth. A man who forgives, receives love, and gives love. A man standing for my own freedom and for the freedom of others.

I may still live in the house of my abuse, but I am no longer defined by its walls.

> God, remind me that I can't change the past,
> but you can enable me to live in the present
> and move into an exciting future.

WHO I USED TO BE

I believe strongly in positive self-talk, that is, in saying true, healthful words to ourselves. Sometimes those words don't feel true when I begin. Part of my motivation is to embrace and affirm the reality about myself that still eludes my emotional grasp.

Long ago, I began to say at least daily, "I love who I am, I love who I used to be, and I love who I am becoming." In the beginning, that was no struggle. But the daily, repeated words forced me to ask myself if I believed them.

Yes, I did love who I am, and I'm excited about the person I'm going to be at the end of my journey. It was the middle statement that began to bother me: "I love who I used to be."

One morning as I was finishing a long, predawn run, that statement seemed to stick in my throat. Immediately, my mind filled with memories of things I had done as a child, and especially those during my teen years. A few adult memories also haunted me.

Had anyone asked, "Have you let go of the past?" I would affirm that I had. I thought that was true—until that moment.

I tried to focus on loving the damaged child I had been, the sad, insecure teen, and even the faltering adult. I knew I *wanted* to love that part of myself.

That morning I gave no triumphant shout of victory. I didn't yell, "Yes! I do." Instead sadness came over me because I held grudges against those younger forms of myself for what they did.

Weeks later, again while running, I said to myself as a child, "I'm proud of you. You weren't perfect, but you survived and you had no one else to depend on." I thought of the angst and immature actions of my teen self. "You did the best you could. You kept going. I love you for doing that because you helped make me who I am today."

With slightly more than three miles left to my run, I sat down on the curb and wept. I had finally treated the younger parts of myself with kindness. I had forgotten how alone he had been—and all of that happened before God took over my life.

"I forgive you," I said and stopped myself. "No! No! I affirm you for doing the best you could. Wrong or right, you were learning to cope in an adult-driven world."

And in that moment, joy filled my heart. I could truly, joyfully shout, "I love who I used to be!"

> Wonderful God, you have always loved every part
> of me. Teach me to accept and love every part of
> myself, especially the person I used to be.

MY IMPENETRABLE SILENCE
Tom Scales

For me, the silence was an impenetrable wall I constructed. It had many uses. As part of my abuse I did many things that, even at the time, were horrific. I definitely didn't want anyone to know the facts. I worked hard to isolate myself from intimate or close relationships. If others knew the reality, certainly they would ostracize me.

The silence about being a survivor of childhood sexual abuse spilled over into other aspects of life. If I didn't want people to find out my secret, I couldn't let them get close in other ways. Open and honest expressions of feelings and emotions were off limits. Anything that would give insight into what and who I really was, I kept under lock and key.

I never developed friendships, much less close relationships. The first responses I got after breaking my silence were so awful and humiliating that I quickly clammed up again.

It took me decades to gain the courage to shed the shame and guilt, forgive myself, and allow God to use those horrible experiences for good in the lives of other survivors.

> Holy God, don't allow me to remain a prisoner of silence. Free me to open up to you and to others.

COMPARING OURSELVES

I spoke with a writer I've known slightly for more than two decades. Back then he had written two books that sold well. When I read his material, I decided he was a much better writer than I, and I'd probably never be as good as he was.

When we talked recently, he said, "I wish I could write as well as you do." When I told him about my comparison (and that I had been a little jealous), we both laughed.

I learned something significant from that interchange. When we compare ourselves to others, we experience negative feelings, and in my case, jealousy. Other emotions arise, such as insecurity and a sense of unworthiness. We focus on what we're *not* instead of who we are. As long as we feel the need to compare, we can't win. We'll constantly see someone who achieves more, gets better breaks, or has greater talent. (Some people compare themselves and feel superior, but that's not my experience.)

A few years ago, I decided not to focus on others' achievements but on my own. I can be only me, and my task is to be the best Cec Murphey I can. Some people are more gifted than I; some are less gifted. My responsibility is to be faithful to who I am and what I can do. I thought of the words of Jesus to Peter. In the final chapter of John's gospel, Jesus tells Peter how he will die. Instead of focusing on himself, Peter points to John and asks, "What about him?"

"What is that to you? You must follow me," Jesus says (John 21:22).

Here's the practical thing I've done. I pray for those of whom I'm tempted to feel jealous. I ask God to bless them as richly as possible. Their success has no bearing on my achievements. The more I champion others, the less I need to compare and the greater my level of inner peace.

Lord Jesus, you don't compare me with others; help me not to compare myself with others, but to be the best me possible.

I HAVE NOT BEEN AS OTHERS WERE

Friendship has always been a large factor in my life. What I didn't get was that *I was usually the good friend*. I pursued relationships, reached out to others, and they responded, but I don't think of them as my true friends, let alone best friends.

That's not to speak against them—but to face the facts. I wasn't able to accept others or be vulnerable to them. When a significant piece of our lives remains hidden from us, as mine was, we don't know how to *receive* such relationships. Even more, we don't know how to *recognize* such relationships.

I reached out for something I didn't have and didn't know how to receive it in return. Maybe that's why I surrounded myself with people. One thing I did realize, even during my teens, was that when I had a serious crisis in my life, I had no one to tell. Most of my life, I lived with that paradox: I had many friends, but I had no true, deep friendship.

When I was still in high school, I read Edgar Allan Poe's poem "Alone" and memorized the first lines because I felt he said it better than I could.

> From childhood's hour I have not been
> As others were—I have not seen
> As others saw—I could not bring
> My passions from a common spring.
> From the same source I have not taken
> My sorrow; I could not awaken
> My heart to joy at the same tone;
> And all I lov'd, *I* lov'd alone.[10]

Why did that poem stay with me and touch me so deeply? I know the answer now, but it was an enigma then. Part of my tortured life was the secret I had told no one until I was middle-aged. Like many other men, my sexual assault kept me isolated and unavailable.

These days I have a best friend and several good friends. I'm open to widening the circle.

Lord Jesus, I felt alone. Misunderstood. Unloved.
Remind me of your everlasting love and sacrifice
for me. You are my truest, most faithful friend.

WHY DO SOME BOYS BECOME VICTIMS?

To some extent, that's unanswerable, but I'll give you my observations. Some boys (and I was one of them) feel unloved and alone. That basic, unmet need to feel loved sets them up.

Every human being yearns for attention and affection. Because a boy doesn't feel loved by his parents or other family members, he becomes susceptible to predators, who shower him with attention and affection. It's part of what we call the grooming technique—when a perpetrator manipulates his intended victim into believing someone cares. Is interested in them. Willing to listen.

Also, the perpetrator generally has some connection to his victim. There are exceptions, but think of it this way. The boy already has a relationship with a family member or someone in the community who is in a position of trust. They might be neighbors, teachers, church leaders, politicians, or a store clerk—anyone whom the boy looks up to, admires, or trusts.

That authority figure befriends the boy and gives him needed attention. The boy feels wanted, accepted, and perhaps loved. The perpetrator would not say it that way, but he (or she) schemes to reach the innocent boy. And if he succeeds, the perpetrator destroys the boy's childhood.

God, remind me that I was one of those needy boys. Someone
with an evil intent took advantage of my innocence. Remind
me that you love me and will never stop loving me.

HIDING THE PAIN

We hide our pain in many ways. The obvious way is by denying it and refusing to admit it. One time, early in my healing journey, I mentioned an abusive experience to a small group and said, "But I'm over it."

One of the men in the small group said, "You're not over it."

"But I am—"

"Your voice and your face show otherwise."

And he was correct. I wasn't intentionally lying, but I was hiding the reality from myself. No one ever asked if I had been sexually molested and physically beaten. That's not a blaming statement, but I had no memories of the sexual assault until I was an adult. One day, while running, the painful memories tumbled out and I couldn't stop them.

In retrospect, that experience of being confronted showed me that I was ready to face my pain. It also told me that all those years I had hidden the pain deep, deep within—so deep I wasn't aware of it.

Shortly after the memories returned, I had a dream. I was underwater and faced a huge cement structure. It was encrusted with seaweed and rust and sealed with a padlock. I wondered what was inside. I pulled at the lock, it broke, and a passageway opened, and I stared inside.

I didn't know what appeared, but I felt something between revulsion and fear grab me. Then I awakened. Later, I realized my dream was telling me that my pain had been hidden and sealed—and had been that way a long time.

The lock was broken and the past had been unlocked.

The pain began.

So did the healing.

> God of all wisdom and knowledge, help me face my hidden pain. Reassure me that you want to heal me.

I CAN HANDLE IT ALONE

In 2004, I recorded a dream in my journal that occasionally still troubles me. In my dream, I helped a man. He thanked me and said, "How may I help you?"

"I'm fine," I said and started to walk away.

"That's your trouble," he said. "You're all for helping, but you're no good at receiving help."

In the dream, I started to defend myself and four other people stood beside him, pointing at me. A woman said, "You don't trust us enough to ask for our help, do you?"

I awakened and grasped the obvious message. I determined that I would let others help me and I'd be more trusting.

Months later, I hadn't done much reaching out for help. Instead, my attitude said, "I can handle it."

The dream, however, reminded me that I was still not able to trust others with my needs. I could blame my sexual assault in childhood, because that's where I lost the ability to be transparent with others. And yet, I'm also still a sucker for people who know how to use the con-artist language. They've taken advantage of me many times, often causing me to lend them money, which they never repay.

But the other kind of trust—the deeper level—when it involves my inner self, I tend to guard it and have been skeptical. As I've struggled over that issue, I figured out one thing. I didn't ask for help because I didn't want to be rejected.

As a child, I couldn't depend on help from either of my parents. On the few occasions when I asked, I was rebuffed.

I grew up learning to depend only on myself. By the time I was in my early teens, I slept at home and ate meals there only on weekends. Other than that, I worked and bought my own clothes and spent my money without consulting anyone.

In my early twenties, I underwent a conversion to the Christian faith, and that helped me in my journey. Yet I've struggled since having that dream. I don't want to hear that accusing voice, "You don't trust us enough to ask for our help, do you?"

I'm learning. Part of my reason for writing books about abuse is that I'm slowly becoming bolder and more honest about myself and my failures.

Gracious God, remind me that even slow is progress.

HOLDING ON

My older daughter, Wandalyn, walked quite early, but she was also fearful. She put her weight on her own feet and, if I allowed her to hold both of my index fingers, she tottered across the room.

One day I had an idea, and I held a clothespin in each hand. She took hold of the other end and we walked. That went on for a few days. One day she grabbed hold of the clothespins and we started to walk. I let go of my end and she kept on walking. Before she reached the other side of the room, she realized what I had done. She dropped the clothespins and after that she toddled around the room on her own.

I tell this story because it works like that for some men in recovery. As long as they have someone to hold on to, they seem to do well. It might be a therapist, a pastor, a support group, a spouse, or a friend.

At some point, they need to walk without holding on to others. When that happens, it means they've overcome their shame and sense of failure. Their self-worth soars.

We also call it maturity, because they can stand on their feet. It's not to say that they don't want others—we always need people—but maturity means we can walk by ourselves and walk *beside* those we trust.

But as long as we hold on by depending on someone else, we don't mature. When we let go and give up the human crutches we might fall a few times. But once we know the freedom and joy of walking without holding on to a safe support, life takes on a deeper meaning because our pain diminishes.

> God, I need people to help me. I also want to learn to walk
> on my own. Teach me to let go and depend on you.

IT COULD HAVE BEEN WORSE

That statement, "It could have been worse," angered me. I heard it only once from a relative. Even though she probably didn't mean it that way, the words were dismissive and minimized the damage the abuse had done. I said nothing.

If I were to hear it today, I'd like to say, "And how much more would it have taken for you to consider it worse?" I'd explain the emotional damage the molestation caused me throughout my life. What did she think would have been worse? If my perp had killed me? Made me a sex slave? (I wouldn't say it, but that doesn't mean I wouldn't want to.)

Most likely I sound defensive here, and she thought her words were encouraging me.

Because of the abusive behavior of others, my childhood was miserable and one time I was suicidal. I felt worthless, unloved, and unwanted. I could add other symptoms, but the question remains: How much worse did it need to have been?

I heard the statement again recently from a man who was trying to share his pain in a small-group setting. And the leader, shockingly, spoke those same words.

After the meeting, the survivor asked me, "Should I go back to that group?"

"You have to figure out that answer for yourself," I said, "but if the leader was as insensitive as you say, I wouldn't go back."

None of us survivors need patronizing words that diminish our pain or make us feel as if we're self-pitying.

Our abuse was bad enough to make us struggle with it all through the rest of our lives. Isn't that bad enough?

Yes, God, it could have been worse. Thank you for
making it better—and that it keeps getting better.

WALKING IN THE RAIN

When Oprah Winfrey still had her daily TV program on ABC, I recorded the second *Oprah Winfrey Show*, which dealt with male sexual abuse, and I watched the program that evening. She invited two hundred sexually assaulted men to be her audience. I was touched by their openness (and their tears).

Afterward, I thought about what I had seen, and I went emotionally numb. I hadn't had that kind of emotional freeze for years. The last time it had happened was when I watched a PBS program on sexual abuse—a documentary by a Canadian woman who had experienced incest from her father. After watching her documentary, I wasn't able to talk and went for a long walk late at night.

A similar thing happened after the *Oprah* segment and I went for a walk in the dark. Even before I was out of my yard, I had a flashback.

I was somewhere between twelve and fourteen years of age. I lived on Second Street but at night I often walked down Third because it was darker and I wanted to be alone. During those walks I felt the pain of childhood—not the molestation because I had forgotten that. I felt useless and unloved.

As I walked, I felt totally alone. "No one cares about me," I often said aloud as I walked. "If I died, I don't think anyone would miss me." I assumed my mother would cry, but she cried about many things, and she would soon forget me.

Walking in the rain caused me to feel even more alone. The rain pelted my face and my clothes, and I didn't care. The brief flashback after the *Oprah* show reminded me of the pain of those teen years. I had forgotten about the walks, but somewhere, deep inside, the memory had lain dormant.

After my walk, I went into our guest room and lay on the bed. I kept thinking of that kid walking in the dark and his pain washed over me again. "I'm with you," I whispered to that confused, miserable teen inside me. "I'm here now and we're both safe."

Eventually I relaxed and fell asleep. Perhaps an hour later I awakened. The pain was gone but the memory remained vivid.

I share this because it reminds me that there seems always to be just a little more hidden pain. But these days, I'm older and I feel compassion for that lonely boy who walked in the dark.

God, there's always another level of pain. Thank you
that each time I overcome, it gets easier.

I NEED TO FIND SAFE PEOPLE

He started his email with admitting he wanted to find safe people. It ended with, "Who are they? How do I find them?"

Those of us in the healing process from sexual assault use the term *safe*. By that we often mean those people who accept us as we are and make no effort to correct our behavior.

Another way to look at it is to say that they don't give us advice unless we ask for it. And even if we ask for it, safe people often hesitate. Sometimes when people ask these questions, they really mean, "Help me find a person who will do the hard work for me."

But truly safe people are those who have known failure, rejection, pain, and other hardships in life—but they haven't given up. They still believe that we can triumph over tragedy and abandonment.

Those people have done the hard work themselves—that's why they're safe. They're usually wise enough to know that they can't provide shortcuts and methods to jump over the pain.

But most of all, those safe people are willing to be by your side while you reexperience the pain.

Savior, help me open myself to safe people—those who
have known their own pain and are open to help.

YOU'RE NOT ALONE

I read those words often, "You're not alone." Sometimes I find them com-forting because it implies that the speaker/writer is reaching out for us. And knowing that we're not alone can be immensely helpful on our journey.

And yet, even though we're not alone because others love and help us, in another sense we *are* alone—a reality we must face.

We do the inner work ourselves; we have to feel the pain, the doubts, and the self-accusations. However, no one in the world knows exactly what we go through.

We are alone because the battle is within—a place others can't go.

Think of it this way. We were victimized in isolation—our perpetrators sought us out, groomed us, separated us from others, and then molested us. Healing means going back into the place of segregation from others. Our problems started there; our victories arise from there.

This isn't to rule out the help of others—and we do need others. But the battle is ours alone.

> God, remind me that, in a very real way, I am
> alone because the battle is within. But you're
> with me so I'm not fighting this by myself.

LESSONS I HAD TO LEARN

About a year after Shirley and I married, I was passed over for a job and I knew I was better qualified than the person they hired.

A day after receiving the news, my mother-in-law, Cornelia Brackett, listened to my moaning for a few minutes. Then she said, "It was probably good for you."

"Good for me?"

Then Mom Brackett said, "I used to worry about you because you're bright and you catch on to things quickly."

"And you worried?"

"Yes, because sometimes you looked down on others who weren't as capable as you are."

I was shocked, and no one had ever said anything like that to me. I pondered what she said and questioned the words. I hadn't ever thought of myself as bright.

In her words I found no comfort, even though I knew what she was trying to get through to me. Years later, after I came to terms with my sexual and physical assaults in childhood, I reminded myself, "Mom Brackett was right. I needed a few failures." Because of those failures and rejections, I learned to reach out to hurting men and comfort them.

Finally, I understood. It's been especially helpful when I began facing my childhood suffering. I'm far from perfect, but I know God has given me a caring, sympathetic heart. I can extend a loving hand or a warm heart *because I know how it feels to hurt.*

Compassionate God, I didn't like suffering or remembering my
hurts, but I know that I can encourage others because I've
experienced pain. Help me to use my experiences to help others.

THE SHAME OF IT ALL

Shame is one of the common elements for us who are survivors of childhood abuse. My definition of shame is that it's a painful feeling of humiliation or distress caused by the consciousness of wrong behavior or *imagined bad behavior*.

My definition means that regardless of who assaulted us, on some level we sensed it was wrong. Individuals older and larger took advantage of us, and we didn't know any better. We were immature children and didn't know what else to do, but we had some awareness—possibly while it was going on or later—even though our perpetrator certainly didn't inform us.

Because of that, as adults we struggle with shame. We have no logical reason for those feelings. We were innocent and powerless. We forget that shame is an emotion and doesn't obey rules of logic.

As an adult, I understand shame is part of our socialization process. Someone said, "No action is required; merely existing is enough." We can't change the feeling, but we can change our attitude toward the effect. I have laughingly said many times, "In our house, we ate shame three times a day."

One day I realized, "I wasn't a bad kid. Those who abused me were bad." The shame didn't disappear, but it troubled me less and less. After that, one of the things I said to myself daily for months was, "I wasn't bad; something bad was done to me."

> God, deliver me from unhealthy shame—the kind
> that holds me back and hinders my growth.

I ACTED OUT

I recently read a romance novel written in 1932. Quaint, of course, but one thing stood out. At the end of chapter nine, the hero picks up the heroine (his wife who had resisted his affections) and carries her into the bedroom. The chapter ends with these words: "He kicked the door closed."

"The next morning," are the first words in chapter ten.

In those days, writers were careful not to write explicitly about sexual issues, but readers figured out what they meant. Maybe that's why we speak of pre–World War II as a time of innocence.

I mentioned that concept because of a phrase I hear quite often today about men who have been sexually assaulted in childhood. They talk about their change of heart, conversion, counseling, and move on to the changes in their lives.

Once in a while, however, a man admits, "I acted out," and that's all he says. I'm certainly not a voyeur, and I'm not interested in graphic descriptions, but I would like more honesty. To say, "I acted out," doesn't truly admit the failure.

Does he mean any of the following?

+ "I fell into sin by . . ."
+ "I was promiscuous."
+ "I've been watching porn."
+ "I had sex with another man."

As repulsive as those statements may sound, they're honest. The men who make these statements acknowledge their failures and sinfulness.

I realize that saying a simple sentence such as engaging in sexual acts, especially with someone of the same gender, is too difficult for some men to admit. Or they may not feel safe in saying those words to someone else.

But if a man seeks healing, at some point he will face the reality of what it means if he "acted out." He learns to speak the truth as candidly as he can. Not to say it straight is a form of denial or at least an attempt to cover its seriousness.

Or it may be a statement still wrapped in shame. He may not be ready to be transparent. I'm not trying to urge survivors to speak openly and publicly when they're not ready. But to speak in euphemisms or catchphrases isn't being straightforward. And rather than aid in healing, it enables men to hide behind empty words.

I'll tell you a powerful lesson I learned in my own healing. Whenever I admit anything about myself *and another person understands what I've said,* I can accept that fact about myself. To state this lesson as a principle: it's still a secret until the survivor admits it to someone else.

Here's a statement I say to myself regularly: "I know of myself only what I say of myself." Once I speak the words aloud to a sensitive, caring person, I've faced my failure. God's grace covers those wounds and sets me free.

Faithful God, help me to openly admit my failures as
I remind myself that you are the forgiving God.

FILLING THE HOLES

Long ago I read the statement that we abused men have holes in our life buckets. Nice imagery. The obvious meaning is that we can never live a full life until we do something about getting rid of the emptiness we face. Many keep trying to fill the bucket, unaware of the leaks from the bottom, and they don't understand why they aren't healed.

What does it mean to stop the leaks? It means getting beyond the symptoms—no matter how much we pour into our healing, we remain unhealed. But if we look at the cause—a hole that may not look big, but it's enough to drain off what we put in—and plug it up, our lives can begin to fill.

For example, in this book I've referred to my drivenness or being an overachiever. Not until I cried out for God to show me what made that hole did I figure it out. Not only did my father beat me regularly, many times he accused me of being lazy. His favorite expression was, "You're like a lazy wart on a log." At the time I faced that truth, my father had been dead thirty-seven years, but I was still trying to prove to him that I wasn't a sloth. That truth set me free.

Repairing the bucket is hard work, and we may have to try to seal it several times before we figure out how to do it effectively and make it last. Sincerely crying out to God gave me the courage to make the repairs. God's repair kit has been sealing the leak slowly and definitely.

> Great, all-powerful God, teach me to look at the
> cause of my pain and not just the effects.

IT JUST TAKES TIME

An old joke goes that a therapist told a man that he'd need to come back once a week for a year. "Could I come three times a week for four months?" he asked.

The joke, of course, is that the man didn't understand how inner healing works. He wanted to rush through the process; there is no rushing through. It takes time. And effort.

For us survivors, we want the healing now and we want to put the torment behind us. Why wouldn't we? Who wants to keep hurting? Perhaps we need to remind ourselves that our abuse took place long ago and the poison permeated every aspect of our lives. We heal, but slowly.

I'm still learning and growing. The good news is that the pain eventually lessens. And my life is far more joyful and contented than it's ever been.

It's worth taking the time.

> God, help me to be patient and self-understanding. Remind
> me that healing is a process—a slow, uneven process.

PTSD

It surprised me the first time I heard sexual assault linked with the idea of post-traumatic stress disorder (PTSD) and yet it fit. Until then, I'd associated PTSD with military veterans who continued to relive their horrible ordeal. When I was a kid, the experts used the terms *shell shock* or *combat stress*.

I made this connection when I read an article about PTSD and learned about those with PTSD having flashbacks and recurring dreams. I said aloud, "That describes many of us abuse survivors."

In my first year of healing, those flashbacks occurred several times a week. I felt as if the assaults were happening all over again. At other times, especially when I faced an extremely emotional situation, I numbed out, which was also listed among the symptoms.

One man wrote me privately and told me about his PTSD and said, "When the flashbacks occurred, I dealt with them by drinking them away. I called it recreational drinking, but I was self-medicating."

For some men, the effect is debilitating. I was fortunate because I'm a full-time freelance writer. For three months after I started my healing, I didn't work much and I stalled on projects. Because the pain and the memories were so new and invasive, I told friends I was just taking a little time off for myself.

I wasn't cured, but during those three months, recurring dreams stopped. The flashbacks came less often, with lower intensity.

We might not think of PTSD in connection with childhood abuse, but there are numerous similarities between the two as well as insights to be gained from comparing them.

> I'm still not fully healed, but I'm getting closer all the time.
> Lord, help me to continue on this path to complete healing.

SAFE BOUNDARIES

In my chaotic childhood, boundaries didn't seem to exist in our family. If any adult wanted anything, we gave it (even though we might have done so with resentment).

Others intruded on our privacy by asking us kids impertinent questions. I now realize they were being inappropriate, and treated us as if we had no rights. It didn't occur to me to refuse to answer.

Years later, I learned something about establishing safe boundaries. The lesson is so simple I've hesitated to express it: I can't set *safe* boundaries without acknowledging my susceptibility. It seems obvious now but it didn't in the past.

The first time I remember closing my bedroom door without fear of being yelled at was shortly after I married. I started laughing, and my wife asked me why. I said, "Now no one can come inside."

When Shirley looked puzzled, I explained that in my home none of us dared close a door or seek privacy. That was the end of the conversation; however, years later, when I began to face my sexual assault, it hit me: I closed the bedroom door as the first awareness of my defenselessness.

Inside that enclosed room, I was safe.

In many ways, I began to face areas where I felt unsafe. I associated that word with *vulnerability*. The word means easily hurt or harmed as well as open to attack. And there's another factor. The word *vulnerable* comes from the Latin word for wound, *vulnus*. After I mentioned the origin of the word, a friend commented, "So once you face the *vulnus*, you are *able* to overcome it." I thought that was a clever way to say it.

"I'm able to heal," I said, "because I'm learning to establish safe boundaries." I'm still learning.

God, you know setting limitations for others isn't easy for me. I need your help to establish wise, loving, and practical boundaries.

VULNERABILITY AND WEAKNESS

For a long time, I was afraid to be vulnerable—I didn't want others to see my weaknesses. If they saw me for who I truly was, they'd surely despise me.

But one day, a group of church leaders in Louisville, Kentucky, held an open discussion on sexual abuse. A recently retired professor from a seminary talked about sexual abuse and defined it exclusively as males penetrating females. *Penetration* was his primary word, which he used several times. When someone asked him about males being molested, he refused to admit that possibility.

Finally, one man stood and said, "Sir, maybe *men* can't be molested, but *boys* can. And they are molested! And your ignorance and closed-mindedness only perpetuate the myth."

Spontaneous clapping broke out before the man added, "I was six years old when I was molested—by my aunt—so don't tell me males can't be abused and I refuse to submit to your macho BS."

More applause broke out. The old professor stared stonily ahead and didn't say another word.

That courageous man who spoke up did so much for me. I had only been dealing with my abuse a short time. It must have taken great courage for him to refute a so-called authority figure.

He isn't weak, I thought. *He's strong.* It takes deep, inner strength to do what he did.

Over the next few days, I pondered that event and realized something: It takes the greatest amount of bravery to be transparent. It took a man of immeasurable strength to stand defenseless in front of two hundred others and expose his painful childhood.

From that time on, I determined to be like that strong man.

> God, it's not easy for me to be transparent.
> Enable me to invite others to see inside me.

REVISITING THE ROOM
Mark Cooper

I realized it was time to ask my Celebrate Recovery sponsor to visit the room where I was abused as a child. I wanted him to see that room. I *needed* him to see it.

"The room" is a bathroom. It's remote, mostly unused, unseen. It appears as if it is in a house that has been long abandoned. For me, that room has been the family secret.

As I led the way, I cried. I was shocked, anxious, and relieved with the choice to allow someone to see the room.

My sponsor stood in the middle of that place and said something I was unprepared for. "Tell me what happened here."

"This is where I was raped."

The room doesn't hold as much power now. By exposing that room, I'm not as afraid of my memories. I don't need to cower in shame from the abandonment that the room represents. The room is no longer my secret.

Lord, "the room" represents a terrible time in my childhood.
Free me from every place, space, or event that still brings agony.

LASTING EFFECTS

The impact of sexual abuse can be devastating and it is long lasting, because you were a child, and you were victimized by someone—and most of the time it was someone you trusted.

The first thing you need to know is this: *the sexual abuse was not your fault.* You may even have been told that you did something wrong, but that person lied. You were a victim; you were an innocent child.

Many adult survivors with whom I've talked told me that they grew up feeling something was wrong *with them.* They believed they caused the abuse and blamed themselves.

One friend said, "If I hadn't been such a good-looking kid, he wouldn't have come after me."

"You're handsome," I said, "but never accept that as the reason—"

"But *he* said—" my friend stopped himself. "When I confronted him, that's what he said."

"Did he ever admit he did anything wrong?" I asked and when he shook his head, I said, "That's blaming the victim. You could have been hideously ugly and he still would have molested you."

So that's first: refuse to accept blame for the pain *and the crime* against you.

Second, find someone who will listen. You may have tried to talk about the molestation and no one responded. Until recent years, too many adults refused to acknowledge that such things occurred. If that happened to you, you have probably felt inadequate, embarrassed, isolated, guilty, shameful, and powerless. Then you probably reacted by suppressing the memory of your rape and it remained a shameful secret.

For example, I was once involved with a men's group. One member, Greg, said that when he was seven, he wanted to tell his mother that his own father was sexually abusing him. One night at dinner, he said, "Daddy has been pulling down my pants and doing bad things to me."

"Eat your dinner," his mother said. His two siblings said nothing; Dad continued to eat.

That was the last time Greg opened his mouth about his abuse until he was thirty-one years old. That's when he joined a group of survivors of male sexual assault.

One day a coworker, who had become a friend, said to Greg, "I'd like to tell you something." He related his own story of abuse and that was the beginning of Greg opening up.

Greg brushed away tears. "Someone heard me," he said.

God, even though my abuse still affects me, I know your
grace and strength will help me overcome it. Help me
rely on your grace and strength to continue to heal.

OVERCOMING THE LASTING EFFECTS

In 2016, I spent four hours with a friend I hadn't seen in more than a year. Weeks earlier he had told me he would be driving through Atlanta (where I live) and asked if I would spend the day with him.

After an hour of do-you-remember-that? he said, "I've read your book on abuse." Sensing he was leading somewhere I nodded, waiting for him to continue.

"I admire you for being so open about—about what happened to you."

After another silence, he said, "Mine was an older boy in my neighborhood." After a lengthy pause, he dropped his head into his hands to hide the tears.

I reached over and put my hand on his shoulder. "I'm sorry."

Three times he started to say something, and finally blurted it out as if it were one word: "I-thought-I-was-in-love-with-him."

He peeked at me and I stared into his eyes. I had no idea what to say because I didn't want to interfere in his battle. My friend was fifty-two years old. "His family moved out of state when I was sixteen. I never saw him again."

After a pause, he stared at me and said, "But I never forgot him. I still think about him."

He gave me a few more details, although I never asked for any. Finally, I said, "And you've been tormented by this for nearly forty years." I said it as a statement.

Vigorously he nodded. "And I know it's crazy. It was wrong. It was sinful, and he did something terrible to me, but . . . I can't forget him."

My friend became a believer during his final year of high school. He went to college and married before graduation. "Paul says it's better to marry than to burn and I was burning . . . for *him*."

Similar to stories of other survivors, he thought that being married would wipe away his lust for the long-ago neighbor.

His marriage has held together—because of a supportive wife—whom he finally told. "But I didn't tell her that the temptation still comes at me." He also confided that I was only the second person he had ever told. "Thank you for trusting me," I said and truly meant it. By then I had tears in my eyes and I realized the years of torment he must have endured.

My friend promised, "I will seek help and I will learn to face my issues."

The last time I heard from him, he emailed, "For the first time in my life, I believe I'm going to overcome this thing."

✦   ✦   ✦

Research now clearly affirms the link between the abuse and the effects. Each of us needs to be able to admit that the long-term effects are powerful and include poor self-esteem, difficulty trusting others, anxiety, feelings of isolation, self-injury and self-mutilation, eating disorders, sleep problems, depression, self-destructive tendencies, sexual maladjustment, and substance abuse.

Your symptoms won't go away. Your pain gets buried deeper and deeper, but you know it's there. If that sounds like you, it means you still need help. "Turn to God" is easy to say, but I add, "and God often works through human skin."

God of grace, help me overcome every bad
effect of my abusive childhood.

I DID IT AGAIN

"I failed."

Such a confession has to be painful. "I did it again, even though I knew better." I read or hear similar statements regularly.

I don't want anyone to fall back into unhealthy or abusive relationships. But they happen. It means that person failed this time—but isn't a lifetime failure.

My friend Patrick has gone back to gay experiences three times in the decade I've known him. After each regression, he swears it won't ever happen again.

Each time I hope not and even now, I pray for him every day. I've been able to say truthfully, "I'm your friend and I care about you. I don't want it to happen again, but if it does, I won't turn my back on you."

Years before I dealt with my sexual assault, I did some work with leaders of Alcoholics Anonymous. One remark stayed with me. "Some people," one leader said, "fail to stay sober and return to AA *several times* before they finally attain ongoing sobriety."

If you're reading this, please, please don't go back to those unhealthy ways. But if you do, it's not a life sentence of failure. Many temporarily fall back.

"My dear children, I am writing this to you so that you will not sin," are the words of 1 John 2:1 (NLT). That's clear; however, I applaud the next sentence, which begins with the word *but*. "But if anyone does sin, we have an advocate who pleads our case before the Father. He is Jesus Christ, the one who is truly righteous."

That verse made me think of Al, who said to a group of us, "I've failed again. My second time. Even finding sexual fulfillment was brief and I hated myself for doing it."

Spontaneously, we all hugged him. One man whispered, "I know how it feels. Welcome back."

Failure is awful. Painful.
But life is filled with opportunities to start again.

> Lord, I don't want to fail. Help me not to fail. But if I
> do fail, remind me that you are ready to forgive.

A NEW SEASON
Mark Cooper

This is day one of a new season. Yesterday I accepted that the word *raped* is my word for what was done to me.

Last night I had a long face-to-face talk with Jason, the man who has been my closest and best friend during my recovery journey.

As he and I talked (I cried of course) and prayed, I took what once would have been a devastating leap. Last night it was a very small and simple (although not easy) step:

> *My name is Mark.*
> *I don't know when, where, or how*
> *But I know I was raped.*
> *And I know my rapist's name.*

For over three years I've had various flashbacks, dreams, vague memories, and body impressions that implicated him. But I wasn't ready to accept that truth until the pain of denial finally outweighed the fear of accepting it.

I don't remember the details of what he did to me, but I know the right word about what he did. It's called *rape*.

When I was young and didn't want to be around him, my mom scolded me and told me how I should feel about him. She didn't explore why I was so set against him. I grew up experiencing tremendous guilt for not liking him, for not wanting to be around him, even as I tried to make myself feel love toward him.

As an adult, I developed a relationship of sorts with him. While he lived, I loved and honored him the best that I knew how. After his death, I wrestled with feeling that I was betraying his memory by considering him as an abuser.

Jesus said, "The truth will set you free" (John 8:32). And it has! The truth that I was raped is ugly. But even an ugly truth brings freedom, whereas a pleasant lie keeps me in denial and bondage. I no longer feel the responsibility to defend him. I'm allowed to be truthful. In speaking truth, I am honoring God, myself, and in a strange way, I am honoring him.

This is day one of my new season.

> Compassionate God, help me see every
> day as a new season of healing.

SAME-SEX ATTRACTION

For most of us survivors, same-sex attraction (SSA) becomes the deepest, most unspeakable secret we heterosexuals hold on to. For me, this is the most difficult meditation I've ever written.

We keep silent because we're afraid people won't understand. Or they'll think we're gay. Or to admit SSA may imply *to us* that we're gay. And many of us live in a culture where gayness is still shocking.

It took me years before I talked to my wife about my own struggle with SSA—not because I acted on those feelings, but the attraction was there. I feared she would think I preferred men.

When I finally told her, she said softly, "I knew."

"You knew and you never said anything?"

"I trusted you." She also said that it didn't trouble her and when I was ready to talk about it, she was ready to hear me.

That was such a relief. I had held that secret deep within for so long, afraid to speak up. And the most important person in my life knew. And even more, she understood.

As I write this, I'm also reminded that a survivor-friend used to say, "You're only as free as your deepest secrets." He meant that as long as we hold back or are afraid to speak up, we're still not healed.

> Dear God, when I share my deepest struggles, that's
> my passage to further healing. Thank you.

NOT READY TO GO PUBLIC

Going public about our childhood molestation is a difficult decision. I never want to be guilty of pushing anyone to do that. But I do consider it one of the major steps toward wholeness.

I've never tried to keep track of the number of emails from men who aren't quite ready. Here's one that came from someone who signed himself as BB and he told me: "I'm not ready to go public and have only told two people about being molested by my uncle. The stories from other men really, really encourage me."

Two things are significant about such responses. First, it's admitting the difficulty of being *ready* to talk about the poisoned childhood. I don't believe in keeping our victimization a secret, nor do I advocate shouting it to anyone who will listen. There is the right time to share.

Second, the fact that they say they're not ready to go public implies they know it's an impending step they'll have to take. I truly applaud that. They're doing whatever they need to do to arm themselves for the day when they can say, "I am a survivor of childhood abuse."

When men finally go public, the healthiest way is to tell a small group of people—individuals they trust and know they would not be pushed away or laughed at by them.

Once I told my wife and my best friend, it still took time before I was ready to tell anyone else. In my case, it was probably a matter of a few weeks (I don't remember exactly). However, I was extremely cautious until I'd told at least a dozen individuals. For most of them, the responses were either a show of kindness or they accepted it as a reality without any significant words.

Now I can easily and freely talk to anyone about my childhood assault.

God, strengthen those who aren't ready.
Guide them until they're ready.

WHY I WENT PUBLIC

I can think of several reasons for going public. First, as long as anything hides inside me, it never gets healed. I'm convinced that God created us to open up to each other to be strengthened by others.

After I admitted to myself the physical, verbal, and sexual abuse of my childhood, the first people I told affirmed me. Those first acceptance affirmations gave me courage to tell others. I can't emphasize enough that we start with safe, caring people.

Another reason is the effect my admission has on others. To my shock, even now years later, I'll be in private conversation and the other person will say something like, "You talk (or write) openly about your childhood. That happened to me too."

Both of us know what *that* means. I respond with something simple such as, "I'm sorry that happened to you."

Sometimes they don't say anything more—not then, and sometimes never. But it opens the door: they told one person, who listened. I like to believe that will embolden them to tell someone else.

When they admit their abuse, and if I sense they want to talk about it, I usually follow up by asking, "Do you want to talk about it?" As important as going public is, I never want to push anyone.

The topic is now as easy for me to discuss as if I mentioned an experience in high school or college. Occasionally I'll laugh and say to friends, "No one can ever blackmail me. It's all out there." Joke or not, I mean it.

Another reason for going public is that if a person can't accept that fact about me, that person doesn't accept me. And I don't want any acceptance based on *in spite of.*

❖ ❖ ❖

I'd also like to point out why it wasn't easy to go public, because I struggled with that. I was afraid of what others might think about me. Would they consider me gay or a deviant? Not want me to be around their children for fear I'd molest them? Would they reject me as unclean or evil?

I'm sure there were other reasons—but they all revolved around what I perceived might be the opinions of others. One day the thought came to me: *If I can't be my total self around them, do I want to be around them?*

Lord, help me be vulnerable and honest about who I am.
You've always known me, and you never stopped loving me.

I DID IT!

Before I could say anything on the phone, Jeremy yelled, "I did it!" I had never heard him sound so excited. "I got help!"

"Tell me what happened."

We met when I lived in Louisville, Kentucky, and he was a member of the church where we worshiped. At the time, I had barely begun to deal with my own childhood trauma and hardly knew how to talk about it. But one time in a conversation, I broached the topic with Jeremy. I can say only that I intuited that he had probably been victimized—although he never said so.

After that he'd frequently ask me about my healing journey, never admitting anything about himself.

After we moved back to Atlanta, Jeremy called me three or four times a year. On one call, he admitted he had been sexually assaulted. When I urged him to get help, he said it was too hard. He said something like, "I'm weak and ashamed. Men aren't supposed to feel that way."

"Maybe not," I said, "but we survivors do. And we stay weak and confused until we get help."

He switched topics and that was all right. The last thing he said before hanging up that time was, "You're a friend. You give me hope."

Slightly more than ten years passed before Jeremy made the exciting phone call to me. He explained how it came about, that he was now involved with a group of men who were also survivors of sexual molestation.

"Why did I wait so long?" he asked.

The only answer I could give him—and I think it's true—was this: "You weren't ready."

Awareness or pain aren't enough. We'll do nothing for our healing until we're emotionally prepared. And all of us have to break through barriers if we want to move forward in our healing journey. For some it's not being able to trust, for others shame holds them back. Regardless of the blockage, when we hurt enough and have to have relief, we'll break through. Or as I like to say it, "When we're ready, we'll start the healing process."

God, make me ready for healing. Remind me that,
for a long time, you've been ready to heal me.

THAT BOY IS MY HERO

Someone, who didn't give his name, wrote to me about his younger self having to make decisions no kid should have to make. "That boy had no one but himself to rely on. . . . That boy is my hero."

I read his email five or six times. He ended it with these words: "I love that boy. When I think of him now, I give him a mental hug, kiss him, and tell him, 'It's okay. I made it. I survived.' I thank him for his ingenuity in keeping me together during a very not-together time in my life. I am proud of him and I tell him so."

What powerful words from another survivor: *That boy is my hero.* And they are words of gratitude that we deserve to give to our younger selves. Because of *our* resilience and courage, we survived. Since then, I've said the same thing several times: "That boy—young Cec Murphey—is my hero."

From time to time I pause and think about my childhood. I hate what happened to me, but like my anonymous writer said, I also smile and remind myself that my younger self is my hero.

I'm reminded that one warm August afternoon, I sat on my front deck and reviewed my life from childhood to adulthood. Still, after all these years, remembering that abusive childhood was difficult and there were times I wondered if staying alive was worthwhile. One time I had contemplated suicide but realized I couldn't kill myself. Thanks, my hero, for surviving.

That day on my deck, I closed my eyes and I could still see my father, belt in his right hand, yelling, "Bend over!"

Then I saw myself standing next to my two younger brothers while Dad cursed me and told me how lazy and worthless I was. He blamed me for my younger siblings not doing their chores.

Immediately my thoughts flashed to the elderly Mr. Lee who sat me on his lap and said, "You're a special boy," as he rubbed my back and my hair. As a child, I believed he cared and was trying to comfort me. But that was only a pretext because he certainly sensed my vulnerability.

Three forms of abuse. And once again, I wondered which was worse. Then I reminded myself, it doesn't matter. *Cec survived.* Today he's strong and healthy because of the resilience of that little boy—still in the formative years of his life—who refused to give up.

My hero.

*   *   *

About a year after I began to face my abusive childhood I read an article about what therapists called the invulnerables. The term refers to those kids who, despite all the obstacles against them in childhood, grew up to become healthy, well-adjusted adults.

That same day I spoke to a female survivor and she said, "Yes, you and I are both invulnerable." We must have talked about that for half an hour. "I'm glad I'm alive," she said. "I survived—but more than survived—I've thrived and been able to use my pain to touch others."

Again today, in writing this chapter, I paused to spend time in prayer thanking God for making that little innocent kid—who had no resources outside himself—able to cope. His younger brothers turned to alcohol at an early age and died from the disease.

Why didn't Cec become like them? How was he able to fight and survive? Above, I wrote *who had no resources outside himself.* That's how I would have described it then. I didn't become a believer until I was twenty-one years old. I also thanked God for being present in my life even though I had no awareness of his presence.

But God was there all along, enabling me to keep going and watching over me.

I *am* an invulnerable and it's because that lonely, neglected, unloved little boy didn't give up. He didn't give up because he, like Joseph in prison, was embraced and loved by a compassionate God.

> Compassionate God, thank you for that boy who is my
> hero. Thank you for giving him the stamina to survive.

DON'T FORGIVE

"I know I should forgive those who abused me," a survivor said. "Should I do it now?"

That's the wrong way to ask. *Should* implies being forced to forgive. Many of our well-meaning friends tend to push us to forgive those who hurt us. And to do it instantly. Sometimes we can't; we still hurt too much.

My answer is simple: "Don't forgive."

That is, don't forgive until you're ready. We've all known men (maybe ourselves) who, under pressure from reading the Bible, hearing sermons, or being nudged by others, say, "I forgive," but they don't let it go.

That was true for me; perhaps it was true about you.

Don't forgive. Immediately. Wait until you've felt the pain deeply.

I advocate feeling sorry for ourselves *for a time*. Some men foolishly say, "I won't forgive. I want them to suffer." Withholding forgiveness doesn't affect them, but it fills our heart with evil poison.

Here's how I did it. I prayed daily for my two perpetrators. I prayed for God to help me *want* to forgive them. I struggled so much over what they had done to me, I felt justified in despising them.

I must have prayed as I did for a few weeks, and one day I thought of the two people. Although both were now dead, I tried to focus on how *they* must have felt. I'm sure they knew what they did was immoral. Wrong. Sinful. Horrible.

So why did they do it? Not everyone agrees with me, but I think they were compelled—I call it an addiction—and molesting a child was a temporary fix for their overwhelming need.

But to call it an addiction or compulsion seemed to dehumanize them. I thought of their inner suffering. I wondered if they hated themselves for what they did. How could they not?

I was finally able to grasp that they themselves had been hurting people, individuals who knew they were doing wrong but seemed unable to stop.

Just to admit that released me. That's when I was ready for healing, and that's when I could forgive them.

Only when we're emotionally ready can we truly forgive.

> Compassionate God, help me be ready to
> forgive those who have hurt me.

HOW DO I FORGIVE?

I can only speak about forgiving my perpetrators from my own view of life. I'm a serious Christian and I try to obey what the Bible teaches me. Jesus taught what we call the Lord's Prayer and that includes a plea for God to forgive "as we forgive." (See Matt. 6:9–13.)

Many people don't go on to read a little further: "If you forgive those who sin against you, your heavenly Father will forgive you. But if you refuse to forgive others, your Father will not forgive your sins" (Matt. 6:14–15 NLT).

The process begins with my sense of being forgiven, just as in the Lord's Prayer we ask God to do that. The next step is that we forgive others. The more I appreciate my own *unearned* forgiveness by God—I call that grace—the more I am able to focus on others who haven't earned the right to have their sins taken away. But then, do we truly earn the right to be forgiven? Isn't it God's loving grace that forgives us *in spite of* what we do? And if we understand that, the *proof of my being forgiven is that I can forgive other undeserving individuals.*

It doesn't have to happen immediately and it may take weeks or months (as it did with me), but if we grasp even a glimmer of grace given to us, we're ready to offer it to others.

This may not work for everyone, but it has worked for me.

> Lord, you forgive freely—and I was undeserving.
> Help me to do the same with my perpetrators.

FORGIVING MY PERPETRATORS

Two people abused me, both of whom were dead before I began to deal with my abuse. I wanted to forgive them, but it took daily, intense prayer. (It may take you only days or possibly years, because we're all different.)

You don't *have* to forgive. Not ever. You can hold the anger and bitterness inside as long as you like. Or you can decide that you don't want to live with such negative emotions eating away at you.

Today most people know that holding grudges, remaining angry for a prolonged period, and unwillingness to forgive mean we—the ones who hold on—suffer.

I don't know how God accounts for sins. The woman who abused me was a prominent Christian and a trustee in her church. I doubt that the old man ever went to church. But I prayed—fervently—that God would enable me to forgive them.

As my next step, I thought of the prayer of Stephen, the first martyr of the church, who prayed, "Do not hold this sin against them" (Acts 7:60). It took a lot of guts, commitment, and love for that man to pray that way for the people who were hurling huge rocks at him until he died.

Although it was biblical to pray that way, it wasn't easy for me. Eventually I was able to pray Stephen's words. I sincerely felt some of their pain and misery. That's not to overlook their awful acts, but it is to say, "God, I forgive them for the terrible things they did to me."

Does such praying do anything for the perpetrators? I have no way to answer that, but it did something good for me: *I was free.*

Forgiving God, help me to forgive quickly and
sincerely. Remind me that I am the prisoner as
long as I allow unforgiveness to control me.

THEY TOO LIVE IN PAIN

I've said that sentence hundreds of times when I refer to perpetrators, instead of seeing them as vile and totally depraved. *They too live in pain.* I started repeating those words to see them as human beings with flaws and virtues.

I sometimes wonder if their pain isn't worse than that of most of us survivors. If they were molested as children (which is true of many of them) not only do they have to cope with those issues, they struggle with the driving compulsion to do to other children what was done to them. It's not that they don't know what they're doing, but I see it as a drive so strong they can't defeat it.

The research and reported experiences point out that it's common for the perpetrators to rationalize their actions. Here's how I define *rationalize*: it's an attempt to provide a reasonable explanation or justify wrong or unacceptable behavior. To rationalize isn't a thought-out action. It's instinctive—an act to save face for unacceptable actions.

What I've written above doesn't excuse perpetrators. And it might even make us angry. I also realize that it means the victimizers probably can't face the heinous crimes they committed so they give themselves explanations to live with their flawed consciences. Perhaps the only way they can live with their actions is to find some way to self-justify. If they faced who they really are—and it occasionally happens—they loathe their actions and hate what they've done.

One former predator said, "After each incident I sat and cried, pleading with God to take away the desire. But it never went away."

They ruin many lives, including their own, even if their victims never tell.

I can never excuse what they did, but I can pity them.

And I can forgive them.

> Lord, help me forgive my perpetrator. He can't be
> whole and healthy while carrying such a load of sin.

TRUTH AND TRAUMA
Tom Scales

I woke up this morning and it was there. Again. After more than sixty years since my sexual abuse happened, the memories came back many times, although less frequently as my healing has taken place.

I refer to the sensation of being sodomized. It's one of the reminders of uglier times.

For decades, the sensation triggered fear, anxiety, rage, and an appetite for revenge. Today, I feel none of those emotions, only a renewed commitment to my participation in programs to protect children and help adults heal from the evil of childhood sexual abuse.

> God, you have healed me and are continuing
> the healing process. Help me do what I can
> to help other childhood victims.

A CONFEDERACY OF SILENCE

Because I was a molested kid and have become a healed adult, I have a responsibility—an obligation—to do what I can to destroy the confederacy of silence that surrounds men who have been wounded by sexual, physical, emotional, and spiritual abuse.

This isn't to make the silent survivors feel guilty. They don't choose to remain silent. It's a self-protecting action for them to remain mute. Too often, they live in silence out of fear that's rooted in shame and believing that others won't listen. Or (and often correctly) they're frightened to speak up because they will not be heard or they'll be rejected if they disclose their horror stories.

Because of fear or shame, they protect themselves, even with those they trust—and that includes those who share their most intimate lives. They're afraid the graphic details of their lives are so horrifying that others who cannot bear to listen will turn away.

Not many safe places or individuals exist for the wounded to share their innermost secrets. They don't know where to turn. Few pastors know how to cope with such situations; friends often feel overwhelmed. Even some therapists aren't equipped to handle such disclosures.

Until we take the risks and bring the dark secrets into the open, a confederacy of silence prevails. For me, the simplest way I know if it's safe is to mention my abuse conversationally.

For instance, I do a lot of teaching among various adult Sunday school classes at the church where I worship. When it's appropriate, I mention my alcoholic father and his beatings and my sexual assault. I don't dwell on the topic. My purpose is to show others that we can talk freely about our freedom from a stolen childhood.

In 2015, I keynoted at a conference for survivors and they gave each of us a small, blue cloth on a safety pin. I forgot to remove mine from my blazer. About a week later I was in church, wearing the jacket.

"What's that for?" a church member asked.

"Oh, I forgot I still had it on," I said and explained that the blue was to symbolize healing for me and for other survivors of sexual assault.

"Oh," he said and moved on.

Instead of feeling rejected, I smiled and thought, *I spoke up. He doesn't have to listen.*

> God, I face a confederacy of silence; I want to
> dismantle and destroy it. Please help every survivor
> to feel safe enough to talk about the past.

MY WIFE AND HER PAIN

Once I crept out of the morass, I realized three important facts. First, I was safe and no longer feared the terrors of childhood. Second, my late wife, Shirley, understood—as much as anyone who hasn't had the same experience could understand. Third—and the most important: *Shirley was the first person in my life who had loved me without demands or conditions.* Because of her, I had finally entered a safe place, grounded in reality. When I wanted to deny that the abuse had really happened, she infused me with courage. When I wanted to quit striving for wholeness, she affirmed me by little things, such as holding my hand or letting me see the tears in her own eyes.

Her unconditional love helped me go through the stages from anger to acceptance and eventually to forgiveness of my now-dead perpetrators.

I'm thankful for my best friend's loving friendship, but Shirley was the person I lived with, and the one individual with the most power to have hurt me. Not once did she reproach me or lash out, and I'm thankful to her for that. The quality of that love enabled me to accept God's unconditional love. Because of her support, I slowly moved forward until I could say, "I know that God loves me, that I'm worthwhile, loved, and accepted by my heavenly Father."

A fourth fact finally got through to me. Over the years, Shirley suffered because of the effects of my abuse. Even now I sometimes feel sad because of the trauma she had to endure, especially during those dark years when she had no idea what was happening. She silently accepted blame for my problems and wrestled with her own issues of self-esteem and failure.

It was unfair, and I owe her so much for being there, for being God's instrument, and most of all for being the human link to hold my hand as I turned to a loving Father.

Dear Lord, I'm sorry I've hurt those closest to me. I can't change what I did, so please help me honor them by the way I live today.

HE'S THE ONE WITH A PROBLEM

Here's another complaint I've heard from spouses. They deny that the abuse has anything to do with them. They can't see how it's *their* problem or that his abuse affects their relationship. That also assumes they don't see themselves having any role in his recovery.

"Fix yourself and leave me out of this," their attitude says.

Or some wives go the other way. They blame all their marital struggles on his sexual assault. Instead of taking responsibility for being a flawed partner in a relationship, they assume every communication problem, struggle, or sexual issue arises as a result of his painful childhood. Thus, if he gets straightened out, they'll have an exceptionally intimate relationship.

Either response hurts a survivor in his movement toward health. The only answer I can suggest is to help his spouse realize: "This is *our* problem. It began with my childhood, but you're a significant part of my life and this involves you as well. I need your help." It also becomes a plea, "Don't turn away from me. I need your understanding."

I also know of several men who've finally had to say to themselves, "I have to do this alone." Their support didn't come from the most significant person in their world. It then becomes his choice whether to find healing alone, or to live in pain and misery with a spouse who won't accept or guide him toward healing.

> Lord, I'm learning that self-healing is no easy journey,
> but it's easier when you and others stand at my
> side. Thank you for being there for me.

DO THOSE THERAPY GROUPS REALLY DO ANY GOOD?

A wife emailed and questioned the value of therapy groups. Talking about her husband, she wrote, "After a therapy session, he comes home sad and hardly talks to me for a day or so. How can that group be helping him?"

Although it was a general question and I didn't know either the wife or the husband, here's how I responded: "It sounds like the group is doing its job. He's facing the abuse. His depression implies that he's aware of deeper issues than he had expected. Please accept that depressive mood as part of the healing process."

I try to remind spouses that healing from the molestation itself is only part of the battle. What were the results of the sexual assault? How does the abuse show up in his adult behavior?

Healing isn't easy and it's not a one-year-total-healing process. It's not comfortable, and none of us signed up for an emotional-memory-erase course. The effects of the theft of our innocence leaked into every phase of our lives. And it demands a long, agonizing journey to heal those parts.

If you're in therapy, hang in there with it. If you're not feeling pain, anger, shame, or some other unpleasant emotion, your group is probably failing you or you're failing to gain from it.

> When I feel depressed or sad after being in a group, loving
> God, help me to realize it can be a positive step in my healing.

I WANT TO MOVE ON, BUT HE DOESN'T

I receive private emails from spouses who tell me they want their husbands to be healed, but the men are reluctant, afraid, or denying their needs.

"What do I do?" they ask.

"Not much," I tell them. "Love him. Assure him of your commitment and don't nag him about getting help." I remind them that healing isn't easy and not every man can hike that torturous trail. In fact, no man will unless the pain forces him.

When I write *forces him*, I mean until the pain becomes so strong and he's so desperate, he feels he must change.

For instance, my neighbor complained about agonizing pain but he kept putting off getting a hip replacement. His doctor didn't push, but he said, "When you can no longer tolerate the hurt, make another appointment to see me." (And that's what happened.)

I also say to the spouses, "Take a good inventory of yourself and your role in the relationship. You may be doing things—overt or subtle—that hold him back. He may be afraid that if he becomes too vulnerable, you'll reject him or turn against him. Or that you might leave him."

To make that stronger, I often ask, "Will you stick with him if he gets depressed or self-absorbed? Will you stay as he deals with his own pain? He may be afraid that you won't."

Lord, like every survivor, I need someone to believe and support me. Most of all, I need my spouse's encouragement. Please remind me that your encouragement is steadfast, and I can always count on it.

FAMILY SECRETS

In our family, sexual abuse wasn't the only thing we didn't talk about. Although no one ever instructed me to pretend, outside the house, we appeared to be an average family with average problems.

But we were liars and frauds by our silence and cover-ups. And yet had anyone said that to my parents or any of my siblings, we'd have been aghast, even angry. The hidden reality was so deeply ingrained in my family of origin, we didn't know a different way to behave.

I broke the silence and brought my sexual assault out into the open. After talking to my wife and friends about my childhood, I gained the courage to talk to my surviving siblings. It was the most difficult conversation I ever had about my early life.

To my amazement (and delight) they were open to me. All of my six siblings are now dead, but we were able to uncover our family secrets before they died. It was as if we no longer had to guard the family's private problems.

Secrets trapped me in the past; now I'm free to live without
secrets in the present. Thank you, Lord, for all the ways
you've helped me deal with my childhood secrets.

COLLATERAL DAMAGE

The term *collateral damage* began as a military term to refer to damage done to civilians or unintended targets in warfare. Today, most of us understand it means the undesired consequences of horrific events. For survivors, it's the harm done to those within our circle, especially family members.

In my own journey, I can think of nothing more difficult for me than when I spoke to my family of origin about the abuse during my childhood and then informed my own children. The first was more difficult because I assumed they, like me, lived with denial. To my surprise, my three older sisters either said, "I knew" or "I suspected."

My own children, again to my surprise, handled it well. The thing I'm grateful for is that I never took my molestation to the next generation— that is, I didn't do to them what was done to me.

I'm grateful I caused no collateral damage for my children.

If you feel you've caused collateral damage, God loves you and forgives you.

> God, if I've caused collateral damage to anyone,
> make me aware and help me repent and change.
> Help me see my mistakes and forgive me.

SECONDARY SURVIVOR

In the previous meditation, I mentioned the other people in my life. I like to use the term *secondary survivor*. That helps to remind me that they're surviving *my* pain and *my* trauma.

My late wife suffered for years because of my unresolved issues. Once I realized that, my attitude and actions changed. I asked her to help me become sensitive to her pain. And she opened up about several things.

A major lesson she taught me was how to set limitations. I had few boundaries in my life. If someone wanted something, I gave it. I loaned money to individuals I knew—even at the time—wouldn't repay me. I'd invite people to our home without considering how it might inconvenience her.

So I watched (and slowly learned) how she handled boundaries. When someone asked for something she didn't want to do or give, she simply said no and gave no excuses. I, on the other hand, occasionally said no and hurriedly added reasons. The other person explained why my reasons weren't valid. If I said, "I don't have time," the response was, "But it will take only minutes a week" and mitigated my statement.

◆　◆　◆

As I became stronger (more healed), I was able to focus on her pain as the secondary survivor. For the last decade of her life, I don't think I ever missed a day (even when I had to do it by phone) of thanking her for loving me and putting up with me.

I never wanted her to forget how thankful I was, and I didn't want to take her for granted as I had over the previous years.

Healing God, help me to be sensitive to the pain of the secondary
survivor in my life. Remind me that she hurts too. Teach me
to give her the affection and attention I want from her.

WHY DOES HE EXPECT ME TO HAVE NO PROBLEMS?

This complaint is more common than I would have imagined. When we who were sexually assaulted begin to heal, we tend to develop the tunnel-vision effect. We're so focused on one thing—our healing—that we shut out others' needs.

I confess that applies to me. In those early days of memories coming back and the intense pain, I didn't have the capacity or awareness to realize that my wife had issues too—and some of them were caused by me.

I'm grateful that she had enough sensitivity to see my hurt and to assume that I wouldn't always be traumatized and self-absorbed. *And I was self-absorbed.* She once compared me to a survivor in a head-on collision. "You survived but you were so damaged, it will take a long time for you to heal."

Not all mates are that compassionate. But I hope those of you who are hurting will take heed. As important as it is to take care of yourself—your primary issue—you also have others in your life. They hurt too. Not in the same way, but they need compassion and patience.

Loving heavenly Father, my tendency is to forget
everything except my pain. Help me to be aware of
the needs of the important people in my life.

PARTNER'S DENIAL

Recently someone wrote about his wife's denial. He told her about his sexual assault. "But she doesn't seem to believe me. She refuses to believe that my childhood memories are real."

I'd call that denial and so did this husband. Sometimes our spouses hear our words, but they can't assimilate the reality that anything damaging happened. They may say things like, "It was such a long time ago," "You were only a child. How could something like that trouble you *now?*" or "Are you still hanging on to that?"

They deny that our abuse mattered. They don't accept or want to admit that the traumatic events of our childhood have a lasting impact. One woman told her boyfriend, "You need to forget that and move on with your life." She assumed that he had a choice in dealing with the abuse—he could let it go, ignore it, or as she essentially said, "Get over it."

If only it were that simple or easy.

By the partner's denial, the survivor's turmoil increases.

Nobody will believe me.

Nobody cares.

I used to say things like, "God cares," but that didn't seem to help the hurting survivors very much. Then I figured out that what they needed (and all of us need) is for someone with human skin to say, "I believe you. I'm sorry for your pain."

In the years I've been writing about abuse, that's the core of my message. I want to be a divine messenger, in human skin, who says, "I care and I want to build a community of other men who say lovingly, 'We understand. We know the pain.'"

> Healing God, remind me that the secondary
> survivor hurts. Make me sensitive to her pain.

I EMOTIONALLY ABUSE MY WIFE

A lengthy email came from a man who had gotten in touch with his abuse in his early fifties. He confessed to emotionally abusing his wife. "How can I stop doing that?"

I don't know the answer, but I offered him a suggestion: *start by being compassionate to yourself.*

Whatever is in our hearts comes out in our actions. Long ago I realized that the people who criticize and speak harshly of others are really letting us peek inside themselves. The way we treat others reflects the way we treat ourselves.

I suggested the emotionally wounded do what I did when I realized some of the terrible effects of sexual, emotional, and physical assault: I admitted I couldn't be truly kind to others until I was genuinely compassionate toward Cec. That meant loving and accepting myself.

I wrote several statements on 3 x 5 file cards and repeated them several times a day.

Here are examples:

+ I am lovable.
+ I am worthwhile.
+ God created me lovable.
+ I like who I am and accept who I am.
+ I lovingly embrace every part of myself.

Weeks passed before the truth of those new messages slowly sank in. Today I can say those words with a smile on my face. I truly like being Cec.

The residual effect has been that as I've become more accepting of myself, it shows up by my being more compassionate and less judgmental of others.

> God, help me show myself compassion.
> Then enable me to pass it on to others.

WHAT IF BOTH OF US ARE SURVIVORS?

I know instances of survivors marrying survivors. In some cases, one of them is aware of the sexual assault and the other starts out in total denial. Either way—knowing before or during the relationship means both partners have a difficult time.

Until the awareness, the spouse who didn't remember or finally faces the past becomes uncomfortable and may try to sabotage the other's healing. It's a normal way to continue denying what they're not ready to face.

And yet, the second survivors sometimes remember their pasts by hearing the other talk about the abuse and the painful memories, the shame, and the lack of self-worth.

Terry told me that he knew about his wife's abuse when they married. "I blamed her for everything that went wrong in our marriage. But I also listened to her. For a time, I also blamed her father for our problems."

Terry stopped talking and wiped tear-filled eyes. "By focusing on her father, I slowly admitted what my own father had done to me. Then I admitted I also had a problem."

Terry stayed in touch with me for nearly two years. The last time I heard from him, he said, "Both of us know we're going to make it. Together."

It is sad, but sometimes both are too wounded to help nurture the other and the relationship falls apart. That's a tragedy, but sometimes they hurt each other too much to stay together.

My friend Lowell told me that he was ready to give up on his marriage and so was his wife until the pastor of their church listened to their stories, befriended them, and helped them start a mutual-help group. "Putting God into the center of our lives saved our marriage. It was our last resort and it worked."

God of grace, you are the unlimited healer. Heal me.
Heal her. Use us to heal others.

WHY DO YOU KEEP GOING TO THOSE MEETINGS?

Pete emailed that his wife nagged him with that question. Others have heard their loved one ask, "Why do you need therapy?"

Sometimes the question is a disguised way of asking, "Am I not enough for you?" The more insecure his spouse, the more this taunts him.

Sometimes the question comes out as, "It seems to me that going to your support group (or your therapist) just keeps reminding you of the past."

Others try to be supportive because they want the pain to go away and they assume—wrongly—that the pain began when the survivor opened himself up and talked about the abuse.

They don't understand that survivors have been hurting since childhood. Now they've identified and focused on the source of the pain. To an outsider, it may seem like paying attention to the problem *is* the problem.

No, other people don't always get it. But focusing on (or facing) the hurt is the big, big step toward healing.

The best answer I can offer is, "I need this for now. I'll stop when I don't."

> Lord, some may not understand why I need to connect with other survivors. But they are part of my healing. Please help them to be patient even though they don't fully understand.

WILL HIS THERAPY CONTINUE FOR THE REST OF HIS LIFE?

I've heard that question often enough. The answer is no—or it can be. We're all different. Some people don't grow or change.

No one can answer the question for a survivor. Those who are getting help largely determine the answer. I was part of a mutual-help group of men for four years before I announced, "You men have been a wonderful source of acceptance and healing, but I think it's time for me to leave."

I felt I was sufficiently healed to go on my own. Not totally healed, but I truly felt they could provide nothing more for me. I offered to stay if they felt I could do anything to help them. Sheepishly, one of them said, "I wish you could. But we're stuck and we'll probably stay stuck a long time." They all agreed that I was ready to move on. I thanked them for giving me the freedom and support to move forward.

I left, and I'm quick to admit that I'm not fully healed. As I continue to learn new things about myself and see deeper into my own soul, the awful, unbearable pain is gone.

As I learn more, I'm able to thank God for the insight I've received. But even more, each enlightening experience helps me to realize that I'm ready for additional insight. Without doubt, those self-understandings come to me *only* when I'm ready to cope with them.

All this is to say that being part of a mutual-help group or under the care of a therapist has an expiration date. That is, when you're willing to put into practice what you perceive about yourself, being on your own may be your next step of victory.

> Therapy isn't a life sentence, but good therapy enables
> me to move forward and enjoy my life. Lord, help
> me to know when I'm ready for the next step.

IT'S NOT ABOUT SEX?

I wonder how many times I've heard the experts say, "It's not about sex. It's about power." Maybe they're right, but I don't think so.

It *is* about sex.

It's difficult for me to believe that my perpetrators came after me because of their powerlessness or their desire to dominate a little kid. Their self-satisfaction had to demand more than to credit themselves with some kind of short-lived control over someone smaller and weaker.

When I hear that oft-repeated statement it seems to lessen the impact of our rape. It was as if they held me at gunpoint and stole my money. Is that also gaining power over another person or does the person simply want my money?

One man who confessed to having molested two boys said, "I had to have it. I could not stop thinking about it. I was driven. There was a deep, inner need I couldn't escape."

Doesn't sound like power to me. Instead, he was overpowered and controlled by a lust he couldn't defeat.

> Gracious God, help me understand that my
> perpetrator was controlled by some powerful, all-
> consuming desire. I was the convenient victim.

I WAS AN OBJECT

Even as an adult, I looked back on old Mr. Lee, my second perpetrator, as a grandfatherly figure. (All my grandparents were dead by the time I was five years old.) I even dedicated one of my early books to his memory.

He didn't love me. To him, I was an object. I was there and he used my body and my soul for his overpowering lusts.

For me to say I was *only a thing* was tough for me. I thought I was special because he often said I was. They were lies.

When I told a friend how hard it was to use the word *object*, he suggested I think of myself as a commodity. He used the word to mean *an article of trade*. He said, "You were like something he bought by carefully grooming you. It wasn't because you were special; it was because you were vulnerable and available."

I hated to hear those words, but they were correct. They helped set me free.

> Lord of life, I was a useful object to him, but you made me a lovable human being. Keep reminding me of that.

EXCUSING

"She couldn't help it," I once said of my female perpetrator. "Her father made her his sexual partner after the death of his wife."

For a long time, I used that as a means to excuse her. "She couldn't help it. It was behavior she learned as a child." That's true, but it doesn't pardon her for sexually assaulting me.

I also excused the old man who molested me. "He was such a lonely man."

More than just excusing the culprits in my life, by defending them (and I was defending), I wasn't pushed to face my anger. But that changed.

Late on a Thursday afternoon, I went for a six-mile run around a small lake and (fortunately for me) no one else was around. That day, my anger exploded.

For at least an hour I raged at the two now-dead people. Just as vehemently, I was angry at myself for defending their actions. After the venom poured out, I allowed myself to grieve over my stolen childhood.

I finished my run, sank onto a bench, and cried for a long time. "I'll learn to forgive you," I said to both culprits, "but right now I want to feel my anger. You hurt me and made my childhood sad and lonely. I didn't deserve what you did to me!"

It was dark by the time I left the park. I didn't feel vindicated or happy. At the time I was worn out, but deep within was the sense that I had faced a harsh, needful taste of reality. I had pronounced them both guilty of murdering the innocence of my childhood.

Now I could focus on embracing that boy who had been deeply wounded. Now I could emotionally hug him for not giving up, and for struggling on. And I shed tears of compassion for that lonely kid.

> Lord, thank you that when I no longer defend the
> guilty, I can have compassion on the innocent.

A REGISTERED SEX OFFENDER

The email below came to me in 2013. I've included it because I want to express compassion and forgiveness for those who committed horrible crimes against us. As terrible as their acts were, a vital stage in our healing (and that of others) is to move beyond our personal pain.

Jesus taught us to pray, "And forgive us our debts, *as we also have forgiven our debtors*" (Matt. 6:12, emphasis mine). Jesus went on to say, "For if you forgive other people when they sin against you, your heavenly Father will also forgive you" (v. 14).

Forgiving our perpetrators is *not* easy, but it means we have grasped that God has pardoned us and because we understand grace, we can learn to do the same for others.

❖　❖　❖

I'm a registered sex offender. I sexually molested eighteen boys before being brought to court. I served a nine-year sentence, and I've been out of prison since December 7, 2009.

While I was in prison, I became a believer. And through the prayers and ministry of other convicts who prayed for me daily, I'm now free. I face temptations, but I *know* the Lord has changed my life, and will help me.

Because I'm registered, I can't hide my past sins or keep them secret, so people know about me. I tried to get involved in two different churches. At the first church, they seemed warm and nice. After a few weeks, I told the preacher and two other people about myself. I figured that they'd find out anyway. After that, they wouldn't even talk to me. It was only a couple of weeks before everyone in the church acted the same way.

One day I came to church late and sat down in the back next to a woman I didn't know. She got up and moved. I walked out of the church and never returned. No one from that church ever contacted me.

In the second church, I didn't have to tell them. They found out after I had been there only a few times. The church board wrote me a letter and said they had had a special meeting about me. They asked me not to come back.

I own a Bible and read it by myself. I watch Sunday services on TV. I've given up on the church. I'm still a believer and I know God has forgiven me. I wish the people of God could do the same.

God, you've set me free from my past. Please help
me forgive those who have sinned against me.

CONFRONT MY PERPETRATOR?

Should I confront my perpetrator? A man needs to decide that for himself. One female and one male abused me and both of them are dead. Even if they were alive, I doubt that I would confront them.

If you feel you want to confront, ask yourself one significant question: What do I want to accomplish? If you want the person to confess, that probably won't happen. Perpetrators usually molest more than one boy and he's probably become an expert in denial. I once read that perpetrators molest an average of two hundred boys in their lifetime.

"I would never do such a thing to you," they often say. "I loved you, but I never did anything wrong." Or worse, they may turn it around and say, "You asked for it. You were always clinging to me and demanding love."

If you feel you must confront, I urge you to take someone with you—someone who can stop your *second* victimization by being accused or twisting the reality. Remind yourself that the perp deceived you once and stole your innocence. He can't do that again, but he can confuse you or bring doubts.

> Lord, give me wisdom. Give me peace and show
> me whether you want me to confront.

YOU ACT SO NORMAL

I've heard that statement in two different ways. The first came from someone with whom I shared my pain. "You're pretty well put together."

I'm not sure what people mean when they say such things. I certainly hope he thought I behaved like a normal person. If I'm emotionally "pretty well put together" it's because I've worked hard to get there.

Another person once said, "I never would have suspected that you had been abused. You're so normal."

Frankly, that's just another dumb thing someone says, probably without thinking. Possibly they're trying to compliment me and their intent is to say, "You have come a long way." Or "You've triumphed over such a painful childhood and I admire you."

Maybe that's what they meant. But it comes across as implying they assume anyone who was abused would remain an emotional cripple.

Regardless, when I hear such things, I say to myself, "He means well and doesn't realize how his words sound." I want to give those people the benefit of assuming they meant well.

I can do that now. But a decade ago, such statements hurt. In those days, such words minimized my journey as if to say, "You're normal so it must not have been too bad."

It's so much easier and healthful to say, "I'm sorry for what you endured." When they say that, I believe they "heard" my pain.

Creator God, I'm not sure what normal is, but I know I'm
growing closer to the person you want me to become.
Thank you for going with me all along the journey.

IF ONLY HE HADN'T

I wonder how many times I've heard the statement from survivors, "If only he hadn't . . ."

None of us survivors of abuse would be where we are if *he* or *she* hadn't done something to us.

It's easy to blame them and say, "It's all their fault." And yes, it *was* their fault. They did it to us. We can stand as accusers every day of our lives and the statement will still be true.

And we'll still be miserable.

Or we can make that our starting point toward healing. If we continue to focus on blame, we trap ourselves in a cycle of negative, destructive thinking.

Why not say the sentence this way? "Even though she . . ." and we focus on our healing journey.

This is where my faith (despite being shaky at times) reminds me of a loving, compassionate God, who desires to heal me. I can point to individuals who embodied the kindness and love I needed and embraced me.

I stand as one sexually, physically, and verbally assaulted kid who has traveled down that healing path. The more I heal, the less I think, "If only he hadn't . . ."

The more I heal, the more I feel I need to reach out with compassion and patience toward others who haven't started the healing journey, or just need a little encouragement to keep going. I also wrote this book, hoping they would share this with their spouses and enlist their loving support.

> God, I know I'm not quite healed, but I'm getting closer. Help me to share my healing with others.

THE BEST WORDS

My healing journey was slow and painful (or so it seems to me) and part of that may be because I live in a culture that expects instant, miracle make-overs. I worked at my healing. I read everything I could find on the topic. I attended conferences where they had breakout groups to deal with sexual issues. I connected on the Internet with men all over the country and a few overseas. I joined a small group of men who affirmed me and loved me.

Nearly three years later, my wife and I were with another couple and Shirley said, "I don't know Cec anymore. He used to be predictable, but he's changed so much, it's like having a different husband." She held my hand, smiled at me, and said, "And I love the new man even more."

Those were the most affirming words I heard during my healing journey. The woman with whom I lived every day saw *and affirmed* the difference.

She asserted what I had begun to feel.

We need the outside witness—someone else to notice and appreciate the change. When that happens, we're able to move further and faster down the healing path.

> God, it's like being born again. My values and
> attitude change because I've taken responsibility
> for my healing. Thank you for changing me.

YOU'RE RESPONSIBLE

In an adult Sunday school, I'd been teaching a series on our bodies being God's holy temples. (The Bible calls them that in 1 Corinthians 3:16–17; 6:19–20.) What surprised me was most class members remained passive about their physical health.

If you have a headache, take an aspirin. Aleve claims to keep it away for twelve hours. Restless leg syndrome? There's a pill for it. Heartburn after eating spicy food? TV screens show several over-the-counter liquids and pills to remove the discomfort.

I noticed the TV ads for prescription medications: many of them end with these words, "Ask your doctor for . . ."

I'm not against medicine or doctors. But I'm against being passive about our physical health.

I am responsible for my health. I have the right—the duty—the responsibility to take care of myself. Too often, the sick passively put themselves into the hands of a professional and look for pills, therapy, or surgery to take away their symptoms.

Instead of immediately seeking a professional, why not start by asking yourself: "What is going on inside me that makes me ill?" For example, instead of taking Tums or Nexium for acid indigestion, why not avoid spicy foods? It's often that simple.

My reason for stressing responsibility is simple. If we truly want healing and yearn to rise above our abuse, we have to work hard at it. Too many men give up and medicate themselves with frenzied activities, antidepressants, or seek the therapist who can set them free.

As an illustration, I'm a professional writer and have taught in more than two hundred writers conferences. One of the benefits to conferees is that they can set up appointments to talk with the staff professionals.

Rarely have I gone to a conference without at least one writer showing me a manuscript that's been rejected countless times. Instead of trying to figure out what they're doing wrong, they keep seeking. One woman said, "I know that one day I'll find exactly the right editor, and I'll sell this book."

She didn't get it. As the saying goes, she keeps doing the same thing hoping for different results. If she truly wants to get published, her task is to find out what publishers want and give it to them. That is, she's responsible to figure it out.

It works like that with healing from our traumatic childhoods. I am responsible.

> Holy Father, I am responsible for my own
> healing from abuse. Thank you that with your
> empowering help, I'm moving forward.

SIDEWAYS ANGER

Most of us struggle with anger on some level. Anger that

- we were molested;
- no one stepped in to save us;
- no one believed us; and
- no one loved us.

Despite the obvious reasons for being irate, some of us don't even know we're incensed. Or I can speak for myself. I had no awareness that I was an angry person. Sometimes the ire popped out—temporarily—but I made no connection that I was an infuriated individual.

If we're angry, it will come out—directly or indirectly. A good way to look at our anger level is to eavesdrop on our own conversation. What do we say about other people? Do we blame the government? Others at work? Those expressions are what I call the sideways anger.

They flow out in unexpected and unrecognized forms such as sarcasm, criticism, speaking our piece, or just being frank.

About a year after I started my healing journey I finally admitted my anger. Part of the slowness of acknowledgment was because I lived among conservative Christians who mistakenly thought it was sinful to be angry. Now I believe they were wrong. The apostle Paul wrote, "'In your anger do not sin': Do not let the sun go down while you are still angry" (Eph. 4:26).

Merely to acknowledge my outrage was a release. I had held it inside for a long time, feeling that if I let go I might kill someone. When I confessed that to my best friend, David, he said, "You're more than fifty years old and you haven't killed anyone yet." That was a marvelous release for me.

Wise and loving God, sometimes I need to be angry, but I
also need to know *what* I'm disturbed about. Help me know.

WHO I AM AND WHAT I DO

I began to focus on my childhood only after I felt loved for being who I was.

As a pastor, I felt loved and accepted by most members, but I assumed it was conditional—based on my performance. It might have seemed a safe environment and perhaps it was. But when I first faced my memories, I asked myself this question: "If I didn't do good things for members of the congregation, would they still love me?"

A few months after I left the ministry to write full time, I finally voiced that question to my late wife, Shirley. She laughed. "That's a distorted viewpoint. You *are* kind and caring. That's part of who you are. *You* may not trust your motives, but people know who you are. You can't hide yourself indefinitely."

My big lesson from that was that I had been safe for a long time, but until I accepted that reality, insecurity and uncertainty troubled me.

> God, I'm learning that who I am and what I do matter to
> you and others around me. Thank you for teaching me.

WHY AM I SO HARD ON MYSELF?

My friends used to tell me that I was too tough on myself. I smiled and replied something innocuous like, "Maybe you're right." I didn't believe them, but that was my way to cut off any discussion on a topic I didn't want to face.

Why couldn't they grasp that I knew my responsibilities and my standards? If I didn't live up to them, why shouldn't I castigate myself? I knew the right thing to do and I didn't always do it.

Like many men who were assaulted in childhood, I grew up with unrealistic self-expectations. (I didn't realize they were unrealistic.) I needed to prove to myself that I was a moral and caring person. Too often, after I failed to live up to my exacting and impossible standards, I sank into a pitiful state, rebuking myself for failing. I had no idea how to show myself mercy—let alone think I deserved it.

How could I show myself kindness when I had received so little of it as a child? Childhood sets us up for adult behavior. In those formative years, I followed the patterns of life around me. Of life in my childhood home.

As I look back, I'm aware that I slowly—very slowly—learned to believe that I was worthwhile and don't have to be perfect. My writer-friend Jeff Adams wrote a maxim that helped me: "Demand perfect; accept excellence."

The odd thing—at least to me—was that I didn't hold others to my exacting standards. I often made excuses for them or reminded myself, "He did the best he could."

The willingness to accept imperfection in others helped change my attitude about myself. One day I was telling my best friend about something I had done and failed. "That was such a stupid and harsh thing for me to do," I said.

David stared into my eyes and said, "It hurts me when you talk like that."

I had no idea what he meant.

"I love you and I don't like you or anyone else saying unkind things about Cec."

I stared at him, trying to grasp what he was saying.

His blue eyes bored into me. "You're kind and compassionate when you tell me about others. But you're mean when you refer to yourself. Don't talk about my best friend that way."

His words truly shocked me, because I hadn't ever thought about things that way. I'd been so careful not to be judgmental about others, especially reminding myself of Jesus' command not to judge others—in the sense of condemning them—in Matthew 7:1, "Do not judge, or you too will be judged." Or as James puts it, "Don't speak evil against each other. . . . God alone . . . is the Judge" (James 4:11–12 NLT).

> Loving God, teach me to be as kind to others *and to myself* as you are. Teach me self-compassion.

I AM A SURVIVOR OF ABUSE

"I am a survivor of abuse." Those six words spoken by those of us who have endured the pain of childhood abuse become powerful when we can finally say them aloud.

The first time I used those words in a public gathering, my heart raced, my hands shook, and the words came out haltingly. But I did it and felt immense relief.

That simple sentence can become a powerful declaration. We aren't perfect; we haven't reached the shores of heaven. But we're stronger than we thought we were. Saying those words has the effect of our shouting, "I am facing the demons of my childhood! I won't give up!"

If you're like me, too often you condemned yourself for being weak, useless, and not like other people. We focused on our failures, on who we weren't. Or we compared ourselves to those who never had the pain and devastation we endured.

We'll never be fully healed, but we can get close. Those six words remind me that following Jesus Christ is a lifelong journey.

◆　◆　◆

I'm not a naturally introspective type. It's easier for me to ignore pain or get busy doing something—anything—so I don't have to look deeply inside. However, as I've focused on saying, "I am a survivor of abuse," no longer do I have to figure out what to do to make people like me. Because I can now say, "I'm a survivor," I'm also learning to say, "I lovingly embrace every part of myself."

Years ago, I was involved with a group of survivors for several weeks. We truly helped each other to stand strong. On the last day, the leader said to me, "You're a survivor. You didn't fail; an adult failed you."

I smiled and thought, *Yes, I am a survivor—but more than that, I'm a victorious survivor.*

God, you helped me admit, "I am a survivor of abuse." I'm not quite healed—but I'm getting closer. Thank you for how far I've come.

BEYOND THE ABUSE

"It's the past. Forget it and move on," my baby brother, Chuck, said to me. We had both been sexually assaulted by the same woman. Although I was Dad's primary victim for beatings and verbal assaults, Chuck was next in line and Dad beat him, especially after I was in my teens and away from home most evenings.

Chuck didn't admit being sexually molested, but he didn't deny it either. On the few occasions when I tried to talk to him about it, he gave me three standard answers to head me off.

"You can't undo the past."

"We don't have to think about those things."

"That stuff happened back then."

His words implied that we need only to forget the past, leave it behind, and it's gone. If only it were that simple. Chuck died after years of trying to cure his pain through alcohol. I don't know if the pain he tried to medicate was the abuse, but I suspect it was.

On rare occasions when he was drunk, he made oblique references to that mess in childhood. "I don't even want to think about those times," he said more than once. Despite his denial, I was convinced that's what he thought about every day and swigging on his beer dulled the pain.

Ostensibly, Chuck wanted to get past the molestation and get on with his life. *So why didn't he move on with his life?*

My second brother, Mel, also became an alcoholic. He was married five times and died of cirrhosis of the liver at age forty-eight. Mel refused to talk about our childhood. "There's nothing back there to remember," was the most he ever said.

I write about my two younger brothers because they seemed determined to move beyond the abuse of childhood by forgetting, denying, or ignoring. Those of us who survive our dysfunctional childhoods know that approach doesn't work.

We don't forget—not really. We don't forget because childhood abuse affects our lives and shapes our attitudes about people and relationships. Part of our healing involves the awareness of our confused and distorted coping mechanisms. They were the devices that enabled us to keep going through the most painful ordeals. But as God opens our hearts and heals, we grasp better ways. We have the power of the Holy Spirit operating in us—if we're open to listen to that sacred voice.

> Lord, it's easy to say, "Forget the past." But it seems impossible not to remember—except when you erase the pain. Help us to listen to your voice as we deal with our past.

EMBRACING SELF-WORTH

Regardless of whether our parents loved or hated us, we survivors didn't *feel* loved. Or wanted. Or cared about. That made us open to perpetrators, who affirmed us (without meaning it).

I had little self-worth as a child. The feeling of laziness and uselessness (according to my father in his angry moments) pushed me to become the overachiever in the family. Here are three unhealthy ways I coped.

First, I got top grades all through school and after I graduated from seminary as the second in my class, I castigated myself for being lazy and not working harder to be number one.

Second, at the time of this writing I've published 138 books. That may sound commendable to many (I used to smile when people marveled at my output). But one day—less than three years ago—the Holy Spirit whispered the words I needed to hear: *You are a driven man.*

And I was. Then.

I'm not sure I'm fully past that, but I'm making progress.

For instance, when I do public speaking and my introduction includes my prodigious output and they list all the other things I've done, I used to smile, delighted to hear such praise.

These days, after the intro, I often comment and say something like this: "Any person who writes that many books is not normal! I was a driven man!" I don't want others to imitate my unhealthy striving for significance.

Here's a third. I lived in Kenya, East Africa, for six years, and the primary name the Africans called me was *Haraka*, which means fast or quick. And I was.

I was frequently praised for learning the language quickly, for working fast and accomplishing much. After my return to the States, people commented on how quickly (and well) I wrote. I beamed. It temporarily made me feel better about myself.

I want to continue to move beyond my abuse, but I want to do it in healthy ways and to honor Jesus Christ. I don't need to be praised for my achievements or my speed (at least most of the time). That, for me, is how I see my moving beyond my painful childhood.

I've learned to like myself, to value who I am.

I'm still not fully healed but I'm far, far down the road from where I was for most of my life. Here is something I say to myself every day and sometimes make it a prayer: everything I am and everything I have come as gifts from God.

Some guys want to hurry and get over it, but it's not something to get over and move on from. *Abuse happened to us.* Until we accept that reality and face how it has warped our values and perception, we're not beyond the abuse. We're still mired in the painful effects. We live—but for many, it's not much more than survival.

In John 10:10, Jesus declares, "I am come that they might have life, and that they might have it more abundantly" (KJV). Other translations, such as the TNIV, read, "and have it to the full." Either translation works for me and each day I seek to live that fuller, more abundant life. As I continue to heal, I am creeping into the fuller life that God offers.

> Lord, remind me that everything I am and
> everything I have come as gifts from you.

PERSPECTIVE
Dann Youle

I felt my sexual abuse caused pain that had no resolution. It seemed like the more I tried to get rid of the pain, the more my heart ached. I felt once again like that lost little boy. Each time the memories would surface, it was as if I were feeling it for the first time. That continued to be the way I felt each time I was aware of it; it's the way I still feel when I remember.

Something changed over time though, and that's been my perspective on the pain.

For the past thirteen years, I've been aware that I was abused after my conscious mind had buried it for almost thirty years. I didn't have a very good perspective on the pain or know what to do with it. Being a person who very much believes that God can use anything in our lives to make us stronger, I still found that *this* anything didn't seem to have much use in my or anyone else's life.

It seemed to be this monster that would rear its big, ugly head from time to time. I don't know when the change took place, but I remember the first time I realized my perspective was changing.

I work for an organization that cares for people at the end of life, and I do direct patient care. If anyone talks about pain, these people have it: physical, emotional, and spiritual. I wondered what was different about the way individual patients dealt with their multifaceted pain. Once I started on my journey of discovery, I realized that for those who had made their peace with whomever or whatever they needed to, their pain lessened. There was much more acceptance of what they were facing. However, those who hadn't made their peace were generally bitter, and had a much harder time accepting the reality of their situation.

The lesson for me has been that sometimes I still let the pain of my abuse make me bitter. When that happens, I can't make peace with anyone. I'm miserable and everybody around me knows it. More often, however, I focus on trying to let it make me better.

When that happens, I'm more at peace and I can fully engage and enjoy life in ways that, even as an almost-fifty-year-old man, I have never experienced before. And that's definitely a better perspective.

While writing about the perspective that I now have of my abuse, the thought occurred to me that stories of how my perspective has changed would be helpful. I want to share one that is the most powerful to me.

On October 28, 2000, a friend and I drove to my abuser's grave in Wisconsin. I remember feeling like there was something exciting but terrifying that would happen that day. We arrived at the cemetery and found it was much how I remembered it, yet strange and different at the same time.

After we searched for about thirty minutes, I saw it. Walking up to the grave, I was visibly shaking and more scared than I remembered being in my life. With my friend giving me my space, but also keeping watch, tears flowed as I said what I needed to say, released forgiveness, and as I sat there, the change started happening.

As I spoke forgiveness toward my abuser, healing flowed. I felt pity for him. I realized he had probably not known he could heal. His generation wouldn't talk about something like this, especially not in a redemptive way. I realized he may have been abused himself. He was probably unable to forgive himself.

Yet from the moment I remembered he abused me, I wanted to get to the point where I could forgive him and myself. My abuser gave me a gift that day, in spite of all the pain he brought to my life and perhaps to the lives of others. He allowed me to see that I could make peace. Peace with him, peace with God, peace with myself, and peace with life.

I could and did walk forward from that day on, knowing that life is a gift. Each day I can truly live and not obsess over something horrific that someone did *to* me and over which I had no control. Now I take charge over this moment, this day, and all the stuff that makes up my life.

That's a perspective change that I couldn't have learned any other way.

Kind and wise God, you have enabled me to change
my perspective. Don't stop now. Keep changing me.

WHY THE MEMORIES AND FLASHBACKS *NOW?*

A few years ago, I read a fascinating master's thesis about men who faced their childhood abuse in what we call middle age—late thirties to early fifties.

Why then? I don't know all the reasons, but I was among those middle-aged types when the reality of my childhood broke through—and it was a painful time for me. For days, I couldn't get past flashbacks and vivid memories.

Why did it take me so long to face the ordeal and the pain of those early years? The most satisfying answer I've found is that it didn't happen until I felt safe. I'd been married to a caring woman for nearly thirty years. Although I use the term *safe*, another way to express it is that I finally understood I was loved for who I was and not for what I said or did.

When I finally grasped that I was loved for who I was without conditions or qualifications, I was ready to face my past.

How about you? When did *you* face your abusive past?

> Caring God, you've always loved me. Help me
> realize I need to do nothing to earn your love.

WHAT DO I WANT?

One of the marks of my healing, although I didn't recognize it at the time, was that I can finally answer my own question: "What do I want?"

Not that I was completely altruistic—always focusing on others—because that wouldn't have been true. But too often I went along with what others wanted without asking myself for my preference.

That turned out to be a big issue for me. It also forced me to realize I truly didn't know what I wanted. Because I felt worthless and shame-filled, it was easier to put up with things than to speak up or to state what I wanted.

Many times, it was as if my preference didn't matter as long as others were satisfied. It's as if I said, "My needs don't matter." (I would never have uttered those words, although that's somewhat the way I felt.)

One of my great thrusts forward was a day when I was still a pastor. I started work early, had nothing pressing me that day, and asked, "What do I want to do today?" No answer came, so I went for a run. Perhaps three miles into my run, my question hit me. *I didn't know what I wanted. I had rarely asked myself. Especially as a pastor and church leader, my role minimized my needs.*

"What if my needs are as important as any member of the congregation?" That simple question was a powerful turning point in my life. "Cec has needs," I admitted, and in more recent days, I love him enough to ask that question regularly.

I still ask. And I'm getting healthier.

> Guiding Holy Spirit, make me aware of my needs. Help
> me to help myself as much as I seek to help others.

SHORT-TERM RELATIONSHIPS

I wonder how many men have written to me, agonizing over their short-term relationships. They speak of anger, distrust, fear, and other significant issues, and then they mention women. "I've never been able to sustain a relationship with any woman," one man said. "What's wrong with me?"

In 2010, I spoke to a man after a meeting in Grand Rapids. With sadness in his voice and on his face, he asked, "Will I ever find someone who loves me no matter what?"

I wish I could have yelled, "Certainly! Yes!"

He was suspicious of people and said it was a big risk for him to talk to me. He stared at the floor for a few minutes before he said, "You only know my first name is John. You'll never see me again, so I guess you're safe."

I nodded, because I understood his inability to trust, although his issue was certainly deeper than the matter of trust. As we talked, he told me about his abuse and then hurried on to say that he had been in six relationships in less than two years. "At first, I was sure each one would last. I wanted each one to be permanent—I really did."

"What happened?" I asked.

"They let me down. They betrayed me and told lies about me." He went into detail about his last affair. As I listened, I realized John wasn't able to acknowledge his fault in anything. He was always the victim.

I could think of many things to say, and I started with a few suggestions. Occasionally he nodded; a few times he smiled. But whenever I paused, he said, "Yes, that's true, but . . ."

After the third or fourth *but*, I stopped. I had been speaking about practical things he could do and I realized that my words weren't what he needed. "May I hug you?" I asked.

He nodded and I warmly embraced him and held him for several seconds. "You don't need instructions," I said. "You need to feel loved and cared for, don't you?"

He pulled away, mumbled his thanks, and hurried away.

Most likely I'll never see him again. That evening I put him on my daily prayer list. I didn't know his full name, but I had a memory of a man with tears in his eyes. I prayed for him daily and fervently for more than six months.

Although I wish I could, I can't do anything for him.

But God can.

And God can use other people in his life.

> Wise God, I realize more and more that people don't
> need my wisdom. They do need my compassion
> and concern. Remind me. Often.

I SHOULD HAVE TRIED

My friend Marlin called early one Saturday morning. He mentioned a man I had known slightly named Hank. "We buried him yesterday," Marlin said. "He was fifty-nine years old."

I wasn't sure why Marlin had called so early, but something in his voice told me it was important.

"Like me, he had been molested—his oldest brother did it to both of us," Marlin said. "Hank didn't talk to me about it and I never mentioned it. But we both sensed that he molested both of us."

Marlin reminded me that Hank had been a civilian who worked for Army Intelligence. "He knew how to keep secrets," Marlin said. "And he certainly kept his own."

His voice broke then and I said nothing until he recovered. "They said he died of a heart attack, and that's probably true, but it wasn't the kind of heart attack that medicine could have treated."

For perhaps ten more minutes, Marlin poured out the story. At first I thought it was his deep grief over Hank's death, and yet I knew they weren't close friends. Near the end of our conversation, he reminded me that he had gotten help through a Celebrate Recovery group. "I wish I had spoken to Hank and told him about the peace and victory I've experienced."

Then I understood. Marlin struggled with guilt about keeping silent. One of the last things he said was, "It might not have done any good, but at least I could have tried."

Those words hit me and I had no idea how to answer him. I had failed other men the same way. Probably like Marlin, I made excuses for myself.

+ "He's not open."
+ "What if he says, 'Mind your own business'?"
+ "What if he says, 'I don't want your help'?"

Those are typical of the excuses I've used. But as my friend reminded me, "I could have tried."

This meditation isn't to invoke guilt or shame—all of us have enough of that. From that day on, I began to pray almost daily, "Lord, if you want me to speak to an abuse survivor and offer help, please guide me. Don't let me have to say to myself, 'It's too late now, but at least I could have tried.'"

Loving God, you know my weakness; you know my hesitancy
to speak to others about their needs. Remind me of what
you've done for me, and teach me to listen to your guidance.

TRUSTING MY GUT

Since 1984, I've earned a living as a full-time collaborator or ghostwriter. Only a decade ago I realized why I've been successful at doing this. Editors tell me I have the ability to get inside others' heads and hearts. Clients trust me, although there's nothing specific I do to engender their faith in me.

Here's an example. A few years ago, I held a retreat for fifteen men. After our first session, Kurt said to me, "You've earned our trust remarkably fast."

That was the first time I'd thought about it. But since then, I see it as my divine gift that developed as a consequence of my abusive childhood. As a young kid, I learned to sense when my dad was working up his anger and would begin beating me—usually a day before he erupted.

I can't attempt to explain how that transfers to adult behavior, but I know it does because I've learned to trust my gut. On two different occasions, I sensed I couldn't work with the people who hired me. But I went ahead anyway, because I couldn't explain the reason to myself for the hesitation. Both efforts bombed.

As survivors, many of us survive and mature because we're willing to trust our instincts. We don't wait for proof or reasons. It's enough to trust our gut instincts.

For me, I realize that self-trust was probably the single biggest weapon I had as a kid. One time a man offered me a ride home in his red Ford after I had come out of a film quite late. In those days, in our city, people didn't think about being molested, robbed, or murdered.

When I told him where I lived, he said he knew the area and we could stop for ice cream along the way. That sounded good, so I got inside the car.

Something didn't feel right to me—nothing I could explain to myself, and he was friendly and seemed nice. But something pushed me to get away. We stopped for a red light and I jumped out of the car. "I'd really like to walk." That's all I said.

A few weeks later, I overheard two of my classmates talking. One of them said someone had given him a ride in a red Ford when he missed his bus. The student went on to say that the man had tried to molest him, but the student was bigger, punched the guy a couple of times, and got out of the car.

I'm sure it was the same man. And I'm sure I wouldn't have punched him. I didn't know God in those days, but years later, I thanked God for his protection. And God used my sense of self-trust.

Teach me, Lord, to listen to my inner wisdom—
a wisdom that comes from you.

I DESERVE COMPASSION

I can now say the words, "I deserve compassion," but it took me a long time to admit. For years, I tried to be self-loving and self-forgiving, but a voice in the back of my head whispered, "You know all the wrong things you did. You've earned your pain."

In one sense, of course, none of us merits anything good in life. (That sentence reveals my theological basis for affirming that every human being is born a sinner.) What I failed to understand is that God has always loved me and has forgiven me. Once I accepted divine forgiveness, I was able to forgive others and feel compassionate toward them. Why couldn't I love and befriend Cec the same way?

Although the process I went through is too complex to relate, for me it came down to this: I didn't warrant compassion until I saw myself as a beloved child of God. If that was true, I didn't have to prove anything or do anything to make myself lovable.

I have three children and I love them very much. If I look at their lives, I can easily point to their flaws or take note of the ways they disappointed me. Instead, I love them and therefore I accept each of them as they are.

The hardest words I recall saying to myself were these: "I am lovable." Although I said them aloud daily, for at least two months, I wanted to add, "because . . ." and list my good deeds. Or I'd have to fight to keep myself from adding, "But look at . . ."

One day, I said, "I deserve compassion. I deserve at least the same level of compassion I would give to anyone else." That was a powerful moment of insight. *I deserve self-compassion.*

I'm lovable; I can show myself compassion. Help
me to be self-compassionate and self-loving.

THERAPEUTIC LEARNING

Years have passed since I initially began dealing with my abuse. I cried so much the first two years I wondered if I would ever stop. And the grief paid off, because I gained insights about my behavior. I call that therapeutic learning.

For example, I realized there were times when I spoke angrily and wasn't even aware of the tone I conveyed.

It still surprises me to gain perspective about myself that stems from the abuse of childhood. I constantly see new ways in which my past changed the way I see the world and react to people.

Another insight for me was facing the fact that I saw my relationships with others as transactions. I gave freely to them, but even though I didn't say it, I expected something in return. And I was hurt when they didn't respond as I wanted.

The more those insights come to me, the more victorious I feel. And even better: the more I like who I am becoming.

> God, sometimes the pain of my childhood
> intrudes and hurts. But thanks to you, even
> the pain turns into therapeutic learning.

LOVE YOURSELF

I picked up a book a few months ago that proposed seventy-five things men could do to find healing from the pain of childhood abuse. Some of the actions and activities were practical.

Some. But not many.

It wasn't that any of the suggestions were wrong; they were just too simplistic. For example, the title of number seventeen was, "Love Yourself."

I agree that's wonderful and much-needed advice. What the author didn't say in the next two pages, however, was *how* to make self-love happen.

How do I learn to love myself? How does anyone?

Answer: I don't know.

My only answer comes from my own experience. Two individuals—my wife and my best friend—loved me without any demands on my behavior. They modeled God's immeasurable love; in spite of my feeling damaged, they accepted me. Neither insisted I go through a course of self-improvement or change my ways. Neither told me to do anything; they accepted me as I was.

They simply loved me. That was the first half of the solution.

The second half was that I *received* their love.

Once I sensed their irrefutable love, I could listen to and empathize with the small, injured boy who lived inside me.

So it's true: if you want to be healed, love yourself. But don't say those words to anyone unless you're able to tell them how. Better yet, express *your* unrestricted love to them. Give your love as an example for them to follow.

Loving God, you love me. Help me love myself.

HEALTHY COPING HABITS

A lot of folks tell men who have been abused to "adopt healthy coping habits."

I always want to shout, "Thank you for that advice. But tell me *how* to do that!" They mean well, but that isn't enough. I'm a pragmatist. Don't simply tell me *what*, tell me *how*.

Most of us who've been abused have figured out that we survived by doing things that weren't helpful or healthful for recovery and growth.

When I began to face my painful childhood, my healthful coping method was to open myself to my own childhood pain. Instead of running from the memories of abuse, I began to do practical things to face them. Reading this book is one great coping mechanism, and inside it you'll find a variety of other ideas on working through your pain, grief, and anger.

Coping with our abuse isn't easy, but it is powerful and life changing.

> Magnificent God, teach me to face my pain
> and teach me your way to heal.

BELIEVE IN YOURSELF

After she insisted I could write a book for her publishing house, and I wasn't sure I was skilled enough, an editor said, "Believe in yourself."

She meant well, and I smiled. At the same time, I wondered, "And how do I accomplish that?"

I want to believe in myself. I want to believe I can win over every challenge. But it feels as if I'm putting together a complicated gadget and no one included the instructions.

Self-belief doesn't come easy for some of us. Braggarts, whom people sometimes mistakenly identify as overly self-confident, too often hide behind powerful words. Inside, they're filled with doubts they try to silence by boasting.

Over the years, I've been learning to believe in myself and vanquish the trauma of childhood. Once in a while, flashbacks hit me (not often and not as severely as they did years ago). Or I'll reflect on something I did and realize I've regressed to an old form of behavior.

But that realization tells me I've made progress. Then I say, "Yes, I'm learning to believe in myself." Even so, I wish people would stop giving me those empty slogans. I've learned to shut up and ignore their advice. One time I did respond to a motivational speaker in a private conversation when he said, "Just believe in yourself."

"Now tell me how."

I embarrassed him and he sputtered for several sentences until I decided to help him save face. "Yes, I know it's my battle, isn't it?"

Perhaps it's yours as well. I don't necessarily have any great how-to advice, but I sincerely affirm that as I learn to accept God's love for me and the affection of others, I believe in myself.

Lord, it's not easy to believe in myself. I'm learning because you've made me teachable. Thank you for your great love for me.

FEELING MY FEELINGS

As I've mentioned elsewhere, my major coping method of survival from abuse was not to feel. When the emotional level got heavy, I went numb. I didn't do that consciously, but it was my way to handle the trauma of childhood. Once I became aware that numbing was what I did, I also realized that I needed to feel my pain—to reexperience the hurts of my past—if I wanted to be free from the past.

Here's how I did it and this may work for others. Each day I said, "God, help me feel my feelings." Followed by, "I feel my emotions." I usually spoke to my reflection in the mirror. I wanted that message to get into my core being.

Although I hadn't talked to a therapist or a pastor, I sensed that facing the hurts and feeling them once again was a step I had to take.

It took months before I became aware of how I felt; it took even longer before I fully accepted the abuse of my childhood. It took years before I knew I had been healed.

The journey wasn't easy, but I refused to give up. At times, I felt alone, unloved, unwanted, unworthy—and other negative emotions flooded through my soul.

Each time I felt my emotions, however, and thanked God for allowing me to experience them, the pain seemed to lessen a little. Now, years later, I can honestly feel my emotions.

Caring God, teach me to feel and to accept my emotions.
You made these feelings, and I want to honor them.

SELF-AFFIRMATIONS

When first exposed to positive self-talk, I was skeptical. I'm still not fully comfortable with some of the practices I read about. Some so-called experts seem to imply they accomplish magical things just by repeating certain phrases. One of them says, "If I can visualize and vocalize, I can realize." Maybe.

What I finally learned to appreciate was that positive self-talk refers to our ongoing internal conversation within ourselves. We do it constantly, and what we say to ourselves determines how we feel and behave. If that's too strong, let's say it influences what we feel and how we behave.

All of us talk to ourselves all day long and we can't not talk. Too often, especially among survivors of abuse, our self-talk is negative, focusing us on guilt about our past or anxiety about our future. But when properly understood, our positive thoughts inspire our actions. If we can redirect the way we think, we can change the actions we take.

As I said, I was a skeptic at first and read widely about self-talk. The most convincing thing I read was that top athletes say they visualize what they want to achieve and keep reminding themselves of it. They also talk to themselves about it.

I tried it and found it helpful, and once convinced, conscious and directive self-talk has been a vital part of my life.

Daily, I repeat self-affirmations or positive self-talk, *but only those that I believe are possible.* They're what I consider reachable goals. Research suggests that if we focus on those possibilities and keep reminding ourselves, eventually our behavior and attitude change.

As an experiment, I decided to focus on my driving. My foot was heavy on the gas pedal and I wanted to overcome that. Each day, several times during the day, I would say to myself. "I am a careful, safe driver. I obey speed limits." Within days, I realized I was staying right at the speed limit.

As I've mentioned, whenever I was overwhelmed with extremely good or bad news, I numbed out. I wanted to experience my feelings, so I began talking to myself about that.

I can't remember when the transformation took place, but months later, I realized that I *was* feeling and I no longer numbed out.

Here's another self-affirmation I repeated for a long, long time and now believe it without having to say it: "I am lovable." I chose that statement for two reasons. First, the Bible makes it clear that God loves us and never stops. For example, "God is love. . . . We love because he first loved us" (1 John 4:16, 19).

Second, I believed it was true intellectually (and could quote many verses in the Bible), but on an emotional level, I had problems. I used to say John 3:16 that tells us that God loves everyone and those who believe have eternal life. My emotional reaction was that I got a package deal. God promised, so he couldn't reject me.

If I repeated a simple fact from the Bible, "God loves me," eventually I would believe it. I did believe it (finally), and no longer need to say these words: "I am loved by God who created me lovable."

The late singer Ethel Waters is often referred to as the originator of this commonly used statement, "I know I'm somebody 'cause God don't make no junk."

I suggest others try positive self-affirmation statements. They can make drastic changes in your self-attitude.

> God, even if it's hard to say I'm lovable, remind me
> that I am lovable because you never create junk.

MY INNER DIALOGUE

A few months after I began my healing journey, I had several dreams one night. In the first, I saw myself as an adult and I held an infant in my arms. I knew it was myself and I said to him, "I'm Cec and you're little Cecil. I'm sorry I wasn't able to take care of you in childhood, but I'm here now."

In the second, little Cecil was maybe six years old. I stroked his cheek and said, "I couldn't help you then, but I'm here now."

In each dream the little child was older. In the final dream, Cecil was a teen. I took his hand and we walked down the street together. "You were so brave," I told him. "You survived and you're healthy. Your brothers didn't make it, but you did. I'm proud of you."

I stopped, turned to him, and hugged him. Then I awakened.

The meaning was obvious, but it started an inner dialogue with me. Even today, years after that dream, I still talk to the boy. I remind him of his survival and thank him for not committing suicide (which he tried to do once).

I like who I am now. I like who I am because that younger self was brave and kept fighting. He didn't let Dad or others defeat him. Growing up, he felt alone and like no one cared.

I'm strong today because he was strong then—even though he didn't realize he was.

All-powerful God, thank you for your strength. Thank you for enabling my younger self to survive his painful childhood.

— *152* —

ME? A CONTROLLER?

I doubt that anyone thought of me as a controller—at least no one ever used that term to my face. But I was and had learned ways of controlling without appearing to do so.

The first time I became aware of that reality was when I met with a group of professionals in the publishing business. We met in a restaurant, where we sat at tables and got to know each other. Within minutes, I realized the other seven people at my table were hesitant to speak up, so I took charge by introducing myself and then asked each one to do the same. After that I threw out questions and kept the discussion moving.

At one point, two of them referred to personal problems connected with their jobs. After a pause, both times I made a humorous comment and moved on to asking why they came to the meeting.

Afterward, I realized I had taken charge of the group. Not that it was wrong; someone needed to do it. But I also admitted that I had manipulated the conversation to keep it on safe subjects—in that case, away from personal problems, especially my problems.

Over the next few weeks I was able to acknowledge that at times I manipulated others and dominated the decision-making process. It was still a long time before I had the insight into my motivation.

Eventually, I faced the reality: I needed to be in control—not that I used that word. I would have said, "I had to speak up." Or "I wanted to keep things on a safe topic." As a child, I had been helpless and powerless and I had that deep, unconscious need *not* to be dominated by others.

I still struggle with wanting to manipulate the outcome. The more secure I am inside, the less I need to dominate. And the more I can trust in a sovereign, loving God.

God, as you make me feel more loved and secure, you
teach me to manipulate others less. Thank you.

REWRITING LIFE

The speaker referred to "strategies for protection from painful memories." He said many of us, unable to face the reality of horrible childhoods, unconsciously rewrote our family history and called that period of life by many terms, such as happy, conventional, nearly perfect.

Yes, I thought, *I was one of them.* In seminary, we had to take courses in pastoral counseling. In a personal interview, the lead professor asked me about my childhood.

"My mother was warm and accepting; my dad was quiet. I had a conventional, happy childhood." I said more than that—and *thought I was telling the truth.*

Years later, I was showering and realized I had not seen my family the way they truly were. "My mother was hard-hearted and unloving!" I yelled at my wife. "My dad was mean and brutal!"

Shirley hugged me and said, "Several times I heard you talk to others about your warm, loving family. I thought your mother was one of the coldest individuals I've ever met."

That opened me up. I had deceived myself (or I could call it lived in denial) and used words like *conventional* or *happy* to express my childhood. From that day onward, I began to accept my real family history. A year later, I could admit that I had been physically, verbally, and sexually assaulted as a child and that neither of my parents expressed affection.

God, help me not to rewrite my childhood history.
Instead, help me to accept the *real* one.

— *154* —

RECEIVING SAFE HUGS

Women have hugged me most of my life, but I was in my twenties when I went to a church where a one-armed man named Benny hugged me. It felt uncomfortable. Over time I learned to receive hugs from men and enjoy them.

An important lesson I learned was the difference between safe hugs and unsafe hugs. My first awareness of an unsafe embrace came at a men's conference. The speaker told us to move around and hug at least five other men.

A man I didn't know grabbed me by the shoulders and pulled me tightly against his body. It didn't feel good and I'm not sure how to describe the difference. I sense that most of us know when bad hugs happen. Maybe he held me a little too long and certainly too tightly.

Not feeling comfortable discussing it with other men at the conference, a few days later, I chatted with three women at church. "Do you feel a difference in the kind of hugs you receive?" I asked.

Without hesitating, all three said they did. "I can tell if a man is trying to hit on me by the way he grabs me." In essence, that's the statement each of them made.

Like me, they were unable to define exactly how they knew, but they did.

That distinction helped me a great deal. A couple of years after that, my wife and I moved from Atlanta to Louisville, Kentucky, for a four-year period. I joined a men's group and became actively involved.

Occasionally I felt unsafe hugs and tried to avoid those men. One of them, Eric, invited me to have dinner with him, and I gave him an excuse. A few weeks later he asked me again, and I turned him down. He didn't ask a third time.

About that time, I heard rumors about Eric being on the prowl for other men. I knew I had made the right decision.

I'm grateful that I sensed the difference. And I think most of us do.

God, thank you for healthy hugs. Keep me away from unhealthy ones.

SKIN HUNGER

All of us need to be touched and embraced. Others took advantage of our neediness and exploited it. We were innocent kids and eagerly accepted affection from anyone.

Regardless of how much help or therapy we receive, the skin hunger doesn't go away. How do we handle it? If you have a spouse, that's probably not a big issue. You touch each other, I assume, with some regularity.

But what if you're single? Or widowed as I am? Needs don't disappear. Perhaps because I've long been one of those individuals who likes to hug and receive hugs, I've been more acutely aware of it.

About a year after my wife died, I noticed ten or twelve gray-haired widows who filled up one pew at our church. I'm not sure what compelled me to do it, but I went up to the woman sitting on the end and said, "I need a hug. Would you give me one?" She smiled and embraced me.

The woman next to her smiled and I said, "I'd like to give you one too." Within a couple of minutes, I had gone down the entire row. I felt good about what had taken place, and it has since become my weekly ritual.

A few weeks later I said to one of them, "Thank you for that hug. I don't get touched all week."

"Neither do I," she said. "And I look forward to your hugs." She was ninety-one years old.

Three more years have passed and I'm still hugging them, and now all of us see it as mutually needed. Best of all, they're safe hugs. We're both responding to that need for a physical, human touch.

That practice has grown beyond the row of widows. I'm now *the* primary hugger in the church and several people tell me that. A woman named Kay runs up to me each Sunday if I don't get to her. "I need my Cec hug!"

I'm delighted to provide that. Men get hugged too. However, I've been careful about the people I embrace. If I'm unsure I ask, "May I hug you?" During the three years I've been hugging, only two or three people said no, and each time I've answered, "Okay, thank you," shook their hand, and moved on.

I focus on this because, as a survivor of childhood abuse, on that unconscious level I needed the skin contact and getting older doesn't destroy it.

Each Sunday when I leave church I've been hugged at least thirty times, possibly even more.

Because those hugs help satisfy my skin hunger, I feel better about life and certainly better about Cec.

Lord, thank you for helping me realize I need hugs.
And in giving them, I also receive them.

KEEP GOING

At a time when I was going through a particularly painful period in my own inner healing, I reread John Bunyan's classic allegory *Pilgrim's Progress*. Near the end of book one, the pilgrim, Christian, must cross the river (death) to enter into the Celestial City. He's terrified, cries out, and wants to turn back. One of his companions says, "You must go through, or you cannot come in at the Gate."[11]

Christian's other companion, Hopeful, stays with him and urges him on, telling him that even though it seems as if he might drown, he won't. "Be of good cheer, my brother: I feel the bottom, and it is good."[12]

Because of Hopeful, Christian makes it to the other side safely. When he gets there, he realizes he was never in any real danger, but fear had caused him to want to turn back. I understood. I had been at the place of despair. I hurt and I was afraid.

As I daily opened myself to those painful memories of childhood, I wanted to give up. I prayed, "God, is it worth the pain?" Some days I didn't feel I could keep going. That section of Bunyan's book gave me courage. I felt as if God whispered, "Don't give up. Keep going forward." I stayed with the pain and I discovered, as Bunyan's character did, that it was solid on the bottom and I wouldn't drown.

Keep going. That's the message. If you read that beloved classic, the message comes through many times in that allegory. One time Christian steps off the path onto a bypath and, once he's aware, he struggles to get back on the right path.

Another time a lion rages at him, and he's fearful but he keeps going. As he gets closer, he sees the lion is chained. It's a direct reference to 1 Peter 5:8–9: "Stay alert! Watch out for your great enemy, the devil. He prowls around like a roaring lion, looking for someone to devour. Stand firm against him, and be strong in your faith" (NLT).

Another factor about the admonition to keep going is that it's not a once-in-a-lifetime temptation. It can come anywhere along the way. And giving up doesn't always happen with intense battles. Sometimes it's complacency or when we sense we're healed enough that we can relax.

If you're committed to a full, wholesome life and the blessings of God, there's no stopping place. You continue to find challenges. And each time, we can smile and say to ourselves, "Yes! It has been worth the effort."

Always-victorious God, give me what I need to keep going.
Remind me that the healed life is worth the struggle.

JUST MOVE IT

As a survivor, I believe strongly in *daily* physical exercise. Most experts on physical fitness suggest some form of aerobic exercise three times a week for about thirty minutes.

Dr. Kenneth Cooper introduced the term *aerobic* in the 1960s and I've been an advocate of his approach since the mid 1970s. He uses the term to refer to exercises that demand the use of oxygen during the workout, such as running, jogging, swimming, cycling, and fast-paced walking.

For survivors, I suggest an aerobic exercise *every day* and as early in the day as possible. (I'm a morning person so that's easier for me.) I chose running, although I now rotate it with fast-clip walking. I used to be able to do fifteen-minute miles walking, but now it takes me one or two minutes longer.

The purpose is to get the heart pumping. Not only does it improve our physical health as Cooper and others have advocated, it improves our mental health, reduces stress, and lowers depression. The experts claim (and so do I) that daily exercise increases our cognitive capacity.

Merriam-Webster defines *cognitive* as conscious mental activities (such as thinking, understanding, learning, and remembering).

For those of us who were victimized as children, this is the easiest and least expensive form of therapy. My daily run doesn't cure anything, but it improves my spiritual and physical outlook.

> Father God, you created our bodies to move.
> Remind me to put my body into action to increase
> my health and my sense of well-being.

POSITIVE EXERCISE

Along with moving the body, something else I've learned is to incorporate positive self-talk while I'm on the move. Combining two powerful forms of self-help—exercise and affirming thoughts about myself—has done amazing things for me.

My rules (which I learned from others) are simple.

1. State facts that are true.
2. Commit yourself to goals you can easily achieve.

For example, I started making two statements to myself:

+ I need to exercise.
+ I will exercise three times a week.

Both were positive and easily accomplished. At times, I had to push myself to do three mornings a week. But once it became habitual, I increased it to five times. Over a period of weeks, I realized how much better I felt about Cec and I was more energetic and creative in my work. And in those days, I was running one mile. Before long I got up to six miles each day—every day.

I kept telling myself the positive effects of those two things. I kept my goal simple and attainable.

Perhaps I sound like a fanatic on this topic. I know only that I've reaped immense benefits and exercise has played a major role on my healing journey.

Lord, thank you that the combination of positive
self-talk and physical exercise is a way you help
me to be emotionally and physically healthy.

THE EXERCISE FACTOR

Just to encourage people to exercise isn't enough. It's a known fact in health spas and gyms that membership numbers peak during the holiday season. But by early February, most of the new members have stopped coming.

One reason people fail with exercise is that they try to make big changes all at once and when they don't succeed, they give up. My advice (and my own experience) says, "Start small. Decide on *one* thing that you can do faithfully. Then add something else."

Next to my faith in a loving God and the positive support of others, I place physical exercise as my best form of therapy and healing. That's because I know what it has done for me. The best way I know to express this is to use myself as an example.

I was born in 1933, so you can figure out my age. Certainly, genetics plays a role, but I'm healthy and exuberant with no physical problems and I take no medication. That's not meant to brag, only to point out what physical exercise does for me.

In 1974, I had been hospitalized twice with ulcers, my blood pressure was in the high normal range, and I was about thirty pounds heavier. My doctor said having ulcers twice made me chronic and he would soon start treating me for my high blood pressure.

I left his office with prayer in my heart and a determination never to have to go back. Just then, a verse flashed through my mind, one I wasn't conscious of having memorized: "Whether therefore ye eat, or drink, or whatsoever ye do, do all to the glory of God" (1 Cor. 10:31 KJV). That verse changed the direction of my life.

I committed myself to caring for my body, God's holy temple. I started with exercise. My first goal was to run half a mile. It took me almost a week to do that. Then I went a full mile.

I never returned to my doctor for the ulcers or high blood pressure—I didn't need to see him. The single most significant benefit was the positive effects on my psyche. Some days I felt sluggish, especially in the early days of my recovery, but I determined to do some exercise every day.

Then I went for a run—no matter how much effort it took to get my feet moving. By the time I came home, I felt good. We sometimes call it the runner's high or we can say the endorphins kick in. Perhaps it's just as important to say that God made our bodies to move and when we do, good things happen.

> Thank you, wise God, that the more I move my body, the better I feel. That's excellent and inexpensive therapy.

ENERGY, ENERGY

I am and have always been a high-energy person, but even people like me have bad days—really bad days. Some mornings it takes immense effort for me to get out of bed and go for a run. Days with rain and freezing weather add another reason to turn over and sleep.

Then I remind myself that I'll feel much better *after* running. And I always do. A few times I drag myself out on the streets early in the morning and I start out wondering why I'm doing it. Even on those days, by the time I'm home and ready for a shower, I *know* why.

I feel better about myself. It's that simple. I don't have to fight negative self-talk or beat myself up emotionally. I realize how blessed I am and enjoy my life more. That's the reason for being able to develop the self-discipline of exercising *every* morning—and it's worth the effort.

I kiddingly say to my friends, "I've saved $300,000 in therapists' fees through exercise."

I'm a self-starter and I realize that some people need others to keep pushing them forward. If that's you, recruit a friend. Get one or two buddies to run or walk with you or stay with you, whatever exercise you choose.

I'm a professional writer and work at home. Almost every morning I see others in my neighborhood exercising while I'm at work. One man and his wife jog (which I use to refer to a slower, more relaxed run). A little later, two wives in their early thirties make the loop in front of my house, which is at the end of a cul-de-sac.

I live 1.3 miles from a high school and sometimes I run there and do a few laps on the track. For the past several weeks, a group of five women has been showing up about the time I get there. They yell at each other, laugh, and I can hear them halfway around the track. They're having fun.

Lord God, help me discover the best way for me to
move my body. Teach me to do it regularly.

IT'S NOT TOO LATE TO HAVE A HAPPY CHILDHOOD

I first read those words as the title of a book by Claudia Black, and I scoffed. "More psychobabble," I mumbled. But the words stayed with me and it took me a long time before I grasped what she meant. (Then I read the book, which I found helpful.)

Obviously, I can't redo my youthful pain; I don't want to rewrite my early experiences. But I can emotionally embrace that crushed, beaten-down, pain-stricken part of me from my childhood.

I've learned to show myself compassion and to understand my defenselessness. Instead of hating that part of myself I'm able to emotionally hold that wounded boy tightly.

Because I've become a strong believer in self-affirmation statements, here's one thing I say several times each morning: "I love who I am, I love who I used to be, and I love who I'm becoming."

And I learned, as Black pointed out, that it wasn't too late for me to heal that traumatized little boy.

> I love who I am, I love who I used to be, and I love who I'm becoming. Lord, thank you for making me the person I am.

BE KIND

At the end of emails to good friends, I sometimes add these words: "Be kind to [their name] today." Occasionally I'll add, "[Their name] is someone I like very much and deserves your kindness."

Not everyone responds and I don't write it to hear from them. I write the words because I mean them. I also write them because I've had to say them to myself many, many times to remind me. When I've messed up, said or done the wrong thing, feel low or lonely, that's when I decide to be kind to myself.

How do I show myself compassion?

My words go like this: "I like Cec; he needs me to support him and he deserves all the love and respect I can give him."

Be kind to yourself.

Say only positive, loving thoughts to yourself. If I occasionally hear myself bordering on negative and self-condemning words, here's what I say, "Cec, I'm sorry I felt that way. You don't deserve the harsh things I've said about you. I promise you that I'll be nicer."

Loving God, today help me be kind to myself.
And tomorrow. And the days after that.

REUSING PAIN

I hate that I was sexually assaulted and physically beaten as a child. So many times, I've wished it hadn't happened. But it did.

Despite the fact that I've been on the healing path for years, I continue to learn about myself and how my painful childhood has carried into my adult years.

One wonderful insight has emerged: I've learned to reuse my pain. That may not be a sophisticated way to say it, but it helps me to think in these terms. Recently, people have said many nice things to me about being a good listener, encouraging them, and being compassionate.

For a long time, I tried to stop them and said, "That's not who I am." I knew my heart, and when I thought about qualities such as compassion I'd grade myself with a C-minus. I'm sure that's because I still struggled with my lack of self-esteem.

Then it hit me. When I was a child, no one listened to me, especially when I tried to talk about serious things. I don't recall anyone encouraging me or expressing tenderness. Perhaps a few individuals did listen, encourage, or express sympathy, but I wasn't aware.

As I've acknowledged those positive qualities others perceive in me, I think of it as reusing my pain. That is, I give to others what I didn't receive. I turn my pain inside out. That wasn't a conscious decision, but it was a healthy reaction to coping with my painful childhood.

Or as the apostle Paul says, "We know that God causes everything to work together for the good of those who love God and are called according to his purpose for them" (Rom. 8:28 NLT). For me, that means he turns my pain into healing and leads me into holy, victorious living.

Lord, thank you for helping me reuse
my pain by caring for others.

LOOKING BACKWARD

When I was living in Africa, early one morning I watched a man with his ox pulling a plow through his fields. The lines were straight and for the twenty minutes or so I stared at him, his gaze never focused anywhere but straight ahead.

I thought of that after I read an inspirational message that urged us not to look backward. Looking backward means going backward, the person implied.

Sounds like good advice in farming, but I'm not sure it's helpful with wounded people like us. We *need* to look backward. That's where our problems began. Unless we go back to the source, we stay busy trying to move forward—but we're dragging a two-hundred-pound bag of rocks strapped to our legs. No one makes much headway that way. Our childhood injuries stay unhealed and keep pace with us.

Going back to that damaged childhood isn't easy. And it takes courage—a lot of courage—to reexperience those wounds and cut away the rocks. But as the saying goes, "The only way *out* is *through*." Meaning that if we want release—true healing—we have to push ourselves to revisit that pain. The big difference is that we can accept our pain and let it help us move forward as mature adults.

We can learn to say things to ourselves like this:

+ I didn't ask for that. I didn't want it.
+ I was a kid with no way to defend myself.
+ That bigger person overpowered me and stole my innocence.
+ I felt unloved and unwanted and someone took advantage of me.

Those statements aren't cure-alls, but they can help us feel tenderness toward that isolated child. Here's a statement I've said to myself many times when I've revisited my childhood: "I did the best I could."

For me, that statement means that I took care of myself through innate but immature wisdom and survived. No self-blame or recriminations. I remind myself that I handled myself the best I could as a six-year-old kid with no one to help him.

Now I can walk—and run—along the healing path.

> Lord, instead of condemning my childhood,
> teach me to say, "I did the best I could."

AFTERWARD

If we continue to move forward in our healing, eventually we reach a place we never would have expected. We can look back and give thanks for our life. It's not that we're glad we were sexually assaulted. But we realize that as terrible as our childhood trauma was, we're actually better people for having gone through the pain.

First, of course, we have to go through the pain—through the shame, guilt, anger, despair, and a myriad of negative emotions. They are parts of our healing journey and, as mentioned in the previous meditation, "The only way *out of* the pain is *through* the pain."

Second, if we continue to move forward, we learn to forgive our perpetrators. And we do that for ourselves. We do it so we can continue to go forward. And for many of us survivors, forgiving may be the most difficult and painful step for us to take.

Third, we finally are able to examine our lives and rejoice in being who we are. I'll tell it as I perceived it. One day I was able to say to God, "Thank you for all I've gone through." I could say that because I had learned important lessons. I was able to feel compassion and tenderness toward others.

How could I possibly have understood what others go through and reach out to them if I hadn't been abused?

That's why I call this meditation *afterward*. It doesn't mean I'm fully healed, but it means I'm maturing and growing in kindness, sympathy, and mercy. I can identify with other survivors and reach out to them in their pain.

And so can you.

Afterward.

If you're not at afterward, may you reach it soon.

Others need you.

> Powerful God, turn my pain around. Heal
> me so I can be a healer to others.

— *Acknowledgments* —

Thanks to my old friend Bill Watkins, who suggested I write this book.

I'm grateful to my agents Deidre Knight and Elaine Spencer of The Knight Agency.

Thanks to my proofreader Wanda Rosenberry who saw so many little things I missed.

I appreciate Dennis Hillman, Steve Barclift, Janyre Tromp, and their crew for standing behind me in putting out my third book on male childhood sexual assault.

Finally, I appreciate and salute the five contributors who show immense courage in providing their names and the facts about their painful childhoods. You guys are my heroes.

Cecil (Cec) Murphey is my name. After the publisher at Kregel Publications offered me a contract, I decided to invite a few other transparent survivors to add to this book. I've known Dann Youle nearly twenty years, since he told me his painful story on the day we met.

In 2009, I met Gary Roe at a writers conference in Seattle. He spotted an ad for my then-forthcoming book, *When a Man You Love Was Abused*, and with much sobbing, he opened up to me. I was the first person he had told.

The other three men I met online. I've never seen Mark Cooper or Roger Mann in person—but I know who they are because of their gutsy transparency. They've also encouraged me. Tom Scales found my blog and contacted me, and we became friends.

I asked these particular men because we care. We want to help. If you want to contact us, we give our information below.

Here's how you may reach me:

+ Go to my blog for survivors and you can post anonymously: www.menshatteringthesilence.blogspot.com.
+ Email me personally at cec.murp@comcast.net.
+ Look me up on Facebook.
+ Visit my website, www.cecilmurphey.com.

Mark Cooper was born in 1968 and has been single his entire life. His recovery journey from childhood sexual abuse and from his own pornography addiction began in earnest in 2011. He is a Christian who values the support he receives from Celebrate Recovery, personal counseling, his church family, and trusted friends. He writes about his healing journey and other topics at www.slingshotscribe.com.

Roger Mann was born in 1949. His father was a preacher and married to Roger's mother until both died in 1995. Roger has been married four years after two previous marriages. Roger has two sons, one daughter, and three grandchildren. He is a Christian who is active in his church and in Celebrate Recovery. He has been in recovery from childhood sexual abuse/assault and various issues that have come from that. His father was his abuser. You can contact Roger by email at mann.roger.a@gmail.com.

Gary Roe's story began with a childhood of mixed messages and sexual abuse. This was followed by other losses and numerous grief experiences. Ultimately, a painful past led him into a life of helping wounded people heal and grow. A former college minister, missionary in Japan, entrepreneur in Hawaii, and pastor in Texas and Washington, he now serves as a writer, speaker, and chaplain with Hospice Brazos Valley in Central Texas. Gary is the author of *Surviving the Holidays Without You* and the coauthor (with *New York Times* best seller Cecil Murphey) of *Saying Goodbye* and *Not Quite Healed*. Gary has been a finalist for several book awards over the years. His other resources include the *Good Grief Mini-Course* and the e-books *Never Alone* and *I Miss You* (available on his website). He also writes columns for several newspapers and is a popular speaker at a wide range of venues.

Gary loves being a husband and father. He has seven children, including three adopted Colombian daughters. He enjoys swimming, corny jokes, and cool Hawaiian shirts. Visit him on the web at www.garyroe.com and on Facebook at www.facebook.com/garyroeauthor.

Tom Scales is a survivor of childhood sexual abuse. He was violated by multiple men and women over a number of years. Through most of his life he suffered nightmares, triggers, substance abuse, and relational issues until he entered a local support group. Through the group and the other members, he learned to trust, process and discard triggers, and find inner peace and joy. He has achieved a level of healing he never imagined possible. As a result of this healing, he has been able to individually mentor hundreds of other survivors. Tom's story is documented in his book *Terrible Things Happened to Me: A True Story of Violence and Victory*. His book received the 2012 Georgia Author of the Year award for an inspirational book.

Daniel (Dann) Youle was born in 1965. He was raised in a Christian home with an older sister and two younger brothers. As a teenager, Dann realized he had same-sex attraction/mixed sexual orientation. Dann married twenty-seven years ago, and he and his wife have walked together through the healing of their respective childhood sexual traumas. They have three young-adult children (two daughters and a son). For the past twenty-five years, Dann has ministered to men who have experienced sexual abuse, sexual addiction, and same-sex attraction. He graduated with his MA in counseling in 2016 and has applied for his counseling license in the state of Michigan. Dann is active in his church and finished his internship with a church in Grand Rapids, Michigan, which has a program called Community Recovery based on the Celebrate Recovery model. Dann plans to center his counseling practice on helping men who are dealing with sexual abuse, addiction, traumas, and same-sex attraction. Dann's abuser was his grandfather. You can contact Dann by email at dann491965@comcast.net.

— *Notes* —

1. See Jennifer Quaggin, *The Other Secret: How to Recover from Emotional Abuse and Live the Life You've Always Wanted* (Bloomington, IN: iUniverse, 2012), 55–56. The statements I wrote in my notebook were originally from a fact sheet from The National Exchange Club Foundation, which Quaggin also quotes.

2. From the Hope for Wholeness website: "We share the freedom in Christ we've experienced from homosexuality, transgenderism, and other forms of brokenness." Visit http://www.hopeforwholeness .org/.

3. "Tyler Perry's Traumatic Childhood," Oprah.com, October 20, 2010, http://www.oprah.com/oprahshow/Tyler-Perry-Speaks-Out -About-Being-Molested-and-the-Aftermath.

4. See, for example, Carol Lynn Martin and Diane N. Ruble, "Patterns of Gender Development," *Annual Review of Psychology* 61 (2010): 353–81, doi: 10.1146/annurev.psych.093008.100511.

5. Kory Floyd, "What Lack of Affection Can Do to You," August 31, 2013, Psychology Today, www.psychologytoday.com/blog /affectionado/201308/what-lack-affection-can-do-you.

6. Gary Roe, *Heartbroken: Healing from the Loss of a Spouse* (North Charleston, SC: CreateSpace, 2015), 72.

7. Gordon S. Grose, *Tragedy Transformed* (Colorado Springs: Believers Press, 2015), 35–36.

8. Ibid.

9. Roe, *Heartbroken*, 46.

10. Edgar Allan Poe, *Complete Tales and Poems* (Edison, NJ: Castle Books, 2009), 837.

11. John Bunyan, *The Pilgrim's Progress* (Peabody, MA: Hendrickson Publishers, 2004), 129.

12. Ibid.

— *Index of Meditations* —

Meditations begin on page 13.

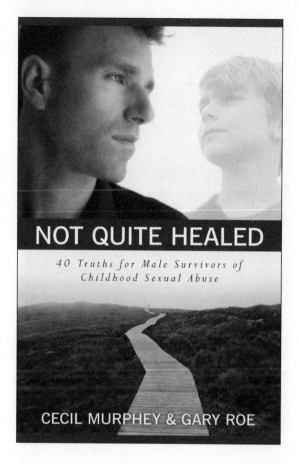

NOT QUITE HEALED

*40 Truths for Male Survivors of
Childhood Sexual Abuse*

CECIL MURPHEY & GARY ROE

Honestly, openly, and empathetically, Cecil Murphey and Gary Roe—two longtime survivors of childhood sexual abuse—respectfully assure you that healing is a process and, by definition, that means it doesn't happen quickly.

But it does happen.

"Cecil Murphey and Gary Roe speak to the heart *and* head of survivors. . . . Here are refreshing words of wisdom for all betrayed!"

—Andrew J. Schmutzer, author/editor of *The Long Journey Home: Understanding and Ministering to the Sexually Abused*

"As a mental health professional for thirty years and founder of the Center for Counseling and Health Resources, I know firsthand the truth in these pages. There is hope and healing for you. You can walk strong again!"

—Gregory L. Jantz, founder of The Center, www.DrGregoryJantz.com

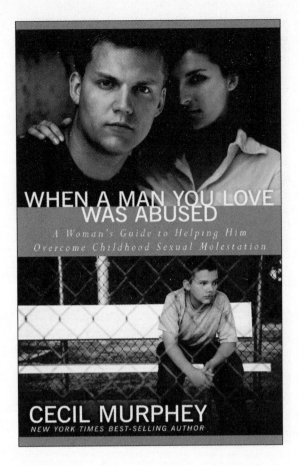

WHEN A MAN YOU LOVE
WAS ABUSED

*A Woman's Guide to Helping Him
Overcome Childhood Sexual Molestation*

CECIL MURPHEY
NEW YORK TIMES BEST-SELLING AUTHOR

An honest and forthright book about surviving—and thriving—despite past abuses, *When a Man You Love Was Abused* offers the encouragement women need to help the men they love towards recovery and healing.

"Murphey's wise and compassionate advice comes from a perspective of victory."
—*Charisma*

"As an abuse survivor himself, Murphey, a New York Times best-selling author, combines balanced, heartfelt compassion and practical steps for healing."
—*Christian Retailing*

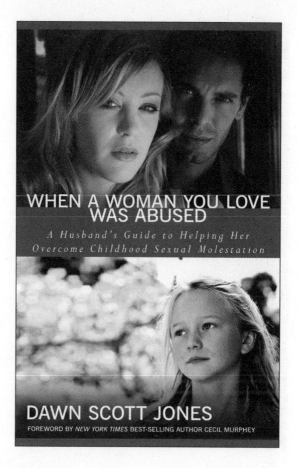

"With insight, perspective, and practicality, Dawn Scott Jones helps husbands tackle the difficult and often unaddressed issue of sexual abuse and walk the road of healing beside the woman they love. Dawn's pastoral ministry and personal experience have uniquely equipped her to write a difficult book on a difficult topic. She writes with honesty, candor, and wisdom, offering true hope for healing and restoration. A book that should be in every church library, pastor's office, counseling office, and retreat center, and used as a resource for men's ministries."
    —Shelly Beach, Christy Award–winning author of seven books, including *The Silent Seduction of Self-Talk*, and contributor to the *NIV Stewardship Study Bible*

"Packed full of important and powerful truth, Dawn Jones's book is an indispensable guide for the man committed to loving a woman who is a survivor of sexual abuse. For him, this realistic yet ultimately hopeful book will be a lifeline. And for the woman he loves, this is the most profound gift imaginable."
                            —Steve Siler, founder and director, Music for the Soul

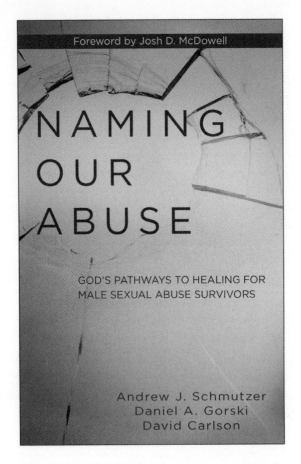

Foreword by Josh D. McDowell

NAMING
OUR
ABUSE

GOD'S PATHWAYS TO HEALING FOR
MALE SEXUAL ABUSE SURVIVORS

Andrew J. Schmutzer
Daniel A. Gorski
David Carlson

"I cannot overstate this: *Naming Our Abuse* is a rare and important book!"
—Joel Willitts, professor of biblical and
theological studies, North Park University

"Silence and shame all too often describe the struggling lives of so many male
survivors of sexual abuse. In *Naming Our Abuse*, these survivors step away from
the world of silence and boldly speak about their unspeakable journeys with the
hope that their collective voices will empower others who are suffering in silence
and shame. These powerful stories bring us that much closer to shattering the
silence and shame that has choked the lives of too many for too long."
—Boz Tchividjian, executive director, GRACE

"Surviving abuse becomes possible when you realize that others who have
endured the same horror are on their way to recovery. . . . This book was written
as an act of love by those who have a heart to reach out to others."
—Dr. Erwin W. Lutzer, senior pastor, The Moody Church, Chicago